for A

Bon ap, vite!!

Dog's
Dinners

[signature]

Dog's
Dinners

A collection of favourite recipes

John Leeson

fantom

publishing

First published in 2014 by Fantom Films
fantomfilms.co.uk

Copyright © John Leeson 2014

John Leeson has asserted his moral right to be identified as the
author of this work in accordance with the
Copyright, Designs and Patents Act 1988.

A catalogue record for this book is available from the British Library.

Paperback edition ISBN: 978-1-78196-106-3

Typeset by Phil Reynolds Media Services, Leamington Spa
Printed and bound in the UK by ImprintDigital.com

Line drawings and cover illustration by Ian Wells

Contents

Introduction

No, this isn't a 'cook book', and I'm not a professional chef; so what's this? It is simply my personal collection of favourite recipes! They've all been cooked by myself and enjoyed across the years, and remain some of my firm favourites.

Some dishes are simple classics requiring no interpretative intervention whatsoever. I have even tried to construct one or two recipes 'off the plate', prompted by memories of notable dishes sampled in favourite restaurants at home and abroad… especially those involving the super-direct flavours of Italy, possibly my culinary spiritual home. I freely admit to being a bit of a thieving magpie as a number of the recipes have been begged, borrowed, or even stolen from good friends or other sources. Like Isabella Beeton herself, you'll find me a bit of a plagiarist!

This collection makes no pretence either to balance or completeness: it is simply 'work in progress' on my part where the key to it all is *taste.*

From the humblest to the grandest I know these recipes work because I have come back to them time and time again, and both my wife Judy and friends who have eaten them seem to like them… quite a lot.

One cannot create a recipe collection without revealing one's own personal tastes and preferences. My options are 'classic British and European' dishes, rather than those on a wider world canvas. These limitations aside, I hope none the less that this collection may prove its worth as an interesting ramble through my kitchen habits!

I am lucky enough to own an AGA™ cooker which provides the warm hub of our house and a magnet in the colder months for our cat to sleep beside. Prestige item though it is, its ultimate flexibility as a cooking machine could possibly be called into question. In the absence of an accurate gas 'regulo' scale, some of my cooking is therefore timed through experience... and I am perfectly prepared to learn from my mistakes!

The tastes are there to be celebrated in the recipes in any event, so experiment and *enjoy!*

John

Starters

Cauliflower panna cotta

A savoury version of the creamy Italian classic. I am indebted to Terry Greenhouse, former *chef de cuisine* of MV *Hebridean Spirit*, for this recipe. A successful savoury twist on an original theme.

1 head of cauliflower
  (as white as possible)
1 pint of milk
1 lemon

1¾ pints whipping cream
8 leaves of gelatine
salt
white pepper

1 Cut the cauliflower head into small florets and place in a pan with the milk and the juice of a lemon. Cook together gently until very soft.

2 Remove the cauliflower from the milk and purée it in a blender until very smooth.

3 Add the puréed cauliflower to the cream and incorporate it well.

4 Place the gelatine leaves in sufficient cold water to soften them to a spongy state.

5 Meanwhile put some of the cream/cauliflower mixture in a small pan and heat through gently without allowing it to come to the boil. Remove from the heat, stir in the

spongy gelatine and stir well until it has completely dissolved.

6 Add this to the rest of the cauliflower/cream and incorporate well. Test for seasoning.

7 Pour the mixture into individual moulds and chill in the refrigerator until fully set, preferably overnight.

Note:

This creamy starter probably cries out for a piquant herb-based sauce. Classic *salsa verde* (see page 37) is an option here. At my last attempt at presenting this dish I added a classic Italian tomato-based sauce, served cold like the *salsa verde*, to give puddles of green and red sauces each side of the white *panna cotta* – the colours of the Italian flag. Pretentious? Certainly. But fun!

A seduction of buttered eggs

'Time and tide and buttered eggs wait for no man.'
– Masefield

No need for a recipe really and only included because, for me, the dish has a romantic history. It was a means of wooing the girl who was subsequently to become my wife! Following the seduction routine of Michael Caine's character Harry Palmer in the film *The Ipcress File* I wanted to say, 'I'm going to cook you the best meal you've ever had...'; and, given my severely limited means at the time, this was it!

Dear bygone days of my youth! Did she only stay with me overnight with a view to a delicious breakfast?

Serves 2 (of course)

4 large free-range eggs	fresh-ground black pepper
(or 6 smaller ones)	salt (to taste)
50 g unsalted butter	

1 Creating this dish requires gentle treatment of the eggs and a minimum of heat under the pan. Go slow for best control.

2 Prepare rounds of good, toasted, buttered bread in advance. (Granary for preference.)

3 In a small pan melt the butter until runny but not hot and fully clarified. Meanwhile crack the eggs into a bowl and break them up with a fork.

4 Remove the pan from the heat and pour in the eggs, stirring them constantly but gently with a wooden spoon. Return the pan to a very gentle heat. Keep stirring until the eggs attain sufficient body to prevent them running loosely, but before they turn into a solidified eggy 'cake'... that's a real turn-off!

5 At this critical point, pour onto freshly buttered toast and season to taste.

Wine:
A breakfast-time Bucks Fizz – why not? Every little helps!

Supplì or arancini di riso

A traditional recipe collected by Lorenza de' Medici in *Italy: the Beautiful Cookbook*.

These stuffed little ping-pong balls of rice make a very good impression on a table of *antipasti*. They are traditional both to Lazio (as *supplì*) and to Sicily as *arancini* – 'little oranges', which they resemble when cooked.

315 g (10 oz) Arborio or
   Carnaroli rice
2 tbsp butter
800 ml (26 fl oz) chicken
   stock
6 tbsp fresh-grated Grana
   or Parmesan cheese
1 egg yolk, beaten

185 g (6 oz) mozzarella
   cheese, cut in small dice
salt, pepper

for deep-frying:
1½ cups of fine dry
   breadcrumbs
vegetable oil

1   Melt the butter in a saucepan and add the rice. Allow to brown while stirring over a high heat for a minute or two.

2   Bring the stock to a boil in a separate pan. Turn the heat under the rice to medium-low and add the hot liquid a little at a time, making sure that it is absorbed before adding a little more. Stir frequently. (A standard *risotto*

procedure.) By the end of about 15 minutes the rice should be fairly dry.

3   Add the Parmesan and adjust seasoning with salt and pepper. Leave to cool completely.

4   When the rice is cold, stir in an egg yolk, making sure it is well distributed. Form into balls about the size of an egg. Push a hole into the centre of each one and insert a small cube of mozzarella into it, enclosing it with the rice.

5   Roll each ball in beaten egg and breadcrumbs. Heat the oil until smoking and deep-fry them until golden brown. Drain, and serve hot, tepid or cold as required.

Variations:

Use well-seasoned sage-infused cooked chopped chicken livers or little chunks of prosciutto, or even a Bolognese *ragù*, in place of the mozzarella if desired.

North Staffordshire oatcakes

I admit I come from marginally further south of Staffordshire itself, so I can't claim absolute authenticity for this recipe. My wife comes directly from the region, however, and confirms these are as close to traditional North Staffordshire oatcakes as a Leicester-born cook like me could possibly make. They are an excellent foil at breakfast time for grilled bacon or boiled eggs.

150 g fine-ground oatmeal	150 ml sour cream
125 g plain flour	2 eggs (large)
1 tsp bicarbonate of soda	salt
2 tsp baking powder	lard, for cooking
150 ml milk	

1   A piece of cake, so to speak. Simply process all the ingredients together in a blender. Transfer the smooth batter to a bowl and allow it to stand for half an hour.

2   Heat a small heavy-bottomed frying pan and add a tiny amount of lard sufficient to grease the entire surface. A heat haze from the pan will indicate the best time to add the batter. Pour or spoon in sufficient batter to make a 6-inch pancake. Bubbles will appear on the upper surface

indicating that the bottom is cooked. Flip the pancake over with a spatula and cook for about a minute. Set pancake aside to cool and proceed as before on the next one.

Little Roquefort tarts

I make these deliciously simple cheese tarts as big as generously sized mince pies. With a cool green salad alongside they are a splendid starter dish for any season.

500 g flaky or puff pastry	2 egg yolks
150 g Roquefort cheese	salt
100 g butter, softened	pepper

1 In a bowl mix together the cheese, the butter, the eggs and seasonings.

2 Roll out the pastry and cut out an equal number of circles of slightly different dimensions – the bigger one as a base and the smaller one as a lid. Butter the separate sections of a bun tray, put in the larger pastry circles and fill each one with the cheese/butter/egg mixture – topping off with the smaller pastry circles, sticking the borders together with a little water. Make a couple of incisions in each pastry top and brush with a little egg yolk thinned down with a few drops of water.

3 Put into a moderately hot oven (gas 6/400 F/200 C) and cook for 20–25 minutes.

Alsace onion tart (Zewelwaïa)

This is just one of many versions of a time-honoured Alsace classic that has the added benefit of being simple to make.

Serves 4–6

225 g shortcrust pastry
1 kg onions, sliced
a little vegetable oil
75 g Gruyère or Comté
  cheese, grated

2 large eggs
salt, pepper
¼ tsp *quatre épices* (see
  page 123), or a scraping
  of nutmeg

1   Make a shortcrust pastry the usual way and use it to line an 8-inch baking tray, or better still a tinned metal quiche tray with a removable bottom.

2   Let the pastry rest somewhere cool whilst slicing up the onions into thinnish slices.

3   In Alsace itself they might well use a little melted goose fat, but I'd suggest pouring a couple of tablespoons of vegetable oil into a heavy-bottomed saucepan, and let it

take heat. Add the onions, cooking them gently until they're a golden brown colour.

4   Remove the pan from the heat, let it cool a little and add the grated cheese, the eggs and the seasonings. Stir well to let everything amalgamate and transfer the mixture to the prepared pastry-lined tray and cook in a moderate (gas 5/ 375 F/190 C) oven for about 25 minutes.

5   Serve hot with new potatoes or cold with a crisp salad and perhaps a cool glass of Alsace Pinot Blanc alongside.

Frittata

Both the Italian *frittata* and the Spanish *tortilla* are relatives of the humble omelette, but are usually served flat. Initially a *frittata* is cooked over a very low heat and then heat is applied to the top via a grill or salamander, leaving it firm and sliceable.

The 'classic' is made as follows:

Serves 4 as a starter

6 free-range eggs (large)
90 g fresh spinach leaves,
　　rinsed, dried and
　　chopped

125 g freshly grated
　　Reggiano Parmesan
　　cheese
a scraping of nutmeg
salt, pepper
1 tbsp good olive oil

1 Heat the grill.
2 In a bowl, crack the eggs and beat them lightly, adding salt and pepper and the nutmeg. Add the spinach and half the quantity of cheese and combine well.
3 In an omelette pan, heat the oil but do not let it start smoking. Add the *frittata* mixture and let it cook *slowly*

over a low heat. Stir the top part of the mixture and allow the bottom part to set and brown in the pan. After about 4 minutes the top part will have formed soft curds and the centre part of the *frittata* will be fairly firm.

4. At this point sprinkle the remaining cheese over the top and transfer the pan to the grill, sufficiently far away from the source of the heat to prevent the *frittata* burning. After about 1½ to 2 minutes the *frittata* top will be gently golden... don't let it burn to a frazzle!

5. Remove the pan from the grill and let the *frittata* cool for a couple of minutes. Put a flat plate over the pan and invert the *frittata* onto it.

6. Let the *frittata* cool down almost completely. Cut in wedges and serve with a simple green salad. An excellent starter!

Warm duck liver mousse

This is my own slight adaptation on Tessa Bramley's 'Chicken liver mousse with bacon and bay leaf', made in the same general way but substituting the richer flavour of duck livers. A classy starter when served with slices of toasted *brioche* and a selection of fine salad leaves.

250 g organic duck livers
milk, for soaking
1 small onion or a couple
  of shallots, chopped fine
2 rashers of streaky
  unsmoked bacon
90 g (3 oz) unsalted butter
a clove of garlic, crushed

a bay leaf
2 sprigs of thyme
1 tbsp Calvados or brandy
1 egg
150 ml (5 fl oz) whipping
  cream
salt, pepper

1   Preheat oven to gas 1/275 F/140 C.
2   Ensure the livers are clean, cut away any greenish spots, and soak in milk to reduce bitterness.
3   Chop the onion or shallots finely, and add the diced de-rinded bacon to them.

4   Melt the butter in a large frying pan and allow the onion and bacon to cook gently until soft, then add the crushed garlic to the pan.

5   Raise the heat and add the livers to the pan to fry briskly with the herbs. Do not allow the livers to overcook – they should still be nicely pink inside.

6   Remove them from the pan.

7   Add the Calvados or brandy to the pan and bring back to a brisk heat, scraping up any meaty residues from the pan itself. Remove from heat and allow to cool slightly.

8   While this is happening, mix the egg together with the cream in a small bowl and add the contents to the pan with the duck livers. Season to taste.

9   Purée the pan contents by whizzing in a blender until smooth, and then pass through a sieve into a clean bowl using the back of a spoon.

10   Pour the mixture either into buttered dariole moulds or small ramekins.

11   Transfer the moulds to a baking dish or roasting tin, and pour in boiling water to a depth of about a third of the way up the moulds.

12   Bake in a pre-heated low oven for about 30–40 minutes, or until the centre of the top of the mousses shows signs of firmness.

Note:

If necessary these can be stored in a fridge until required, covered with cling film. Simply transfer the covered moulds to a steamer until warmed through thoroughly, and serve directly from the moulds surrounded by salad leaves and with toast or *brioche*.

Goat's cheese and hazelnut soufflés

A recipe from Joyce Molyneux, formerly of the Carved Angel restaurant, Dartmouth, Devon.

Serves 8

50 g butter
50 g flour
300 ml single cream
300 ml milk
1 tsp chopped fresh thyme
1 pinch grated nutmeg
4 egg yolks
6 egg whites

225 g soft goat's cheese
a little melted butter
2 tbsp dry breadcrumbs
2 tbsp grated Parmesan
  cheese
50 g roasted hazelnuts,
  coarsely chopped
salt, pepper

1   Make a *roux* with the butter and flour, then add the milk and cream and cook the sauce gently for 4 or 5 minutes. Season it with salt and pepper and add the thyme and the nutmeg. Set the sauce aside to cool, then add the egg yolks and the goat's cheese. Whip the egg whites until stiff and fold them into the sauce.

2 Preheat the oven to gas 7/425 F/220 C. Meanwhile brush the insides of eight 10 cm ramekin dishes with melted butter. Mix together the breadcrumbs and the Parmesan cheese and coat the insides of the ramekins.

3 Fill the ramekins about three-quarters full with the soufflé mixture, scatter some chopped roast hazelnuts on the top and cook in the oven for about 10–15 minutes. Serve with a dressed salad.

Twice-cooked pimento soufflé 'Suissesse'

Yet another delicious starter recipe from the earlier days of Dartmouth's Carved Angel.

Serves 4

1 pimento, diced
150 ml milk
25 g butter
½ clove garlic
25 g flour
salt, pepper

1 tablespoon Parmesan
  cheese
chopped parsley
2 eggs, separated
150 ml double cream

1   Heat the milk with half the diced pimento to scalding point then whizz in a blender.
2   In a pan, melt the butter and add the flour, seasoning and the Parmesan cheese and cook, stirring, for a few minutes.
3   Pour on the milk mixture and add the chopped parsley. Beat together well and then allow to cool slightly.
4   Add the egg yolks, and beat well to combine.

5   Whisk the egg whites and gently fold them into the mixture.

6   Divide between 4 buttered ramekins and cook in a bain-marie filled with boiling water to come halfway up their sides for 20 minutes at gas 7/425 F/220 C.

7   Remove from the oven and, when cooled down sufficiently to handle, turn them out individually onto ovenproof dishes.

8   Prior to serving them, pour over the cream, sprinkle with a little more Parmesan, and bake in a hot oven for 6 minutes. Serve immediately.

Pasticcio al erbette:
a herb-infused terrine

A recipe to prove your 'green' credentials – up to a point! Although its meat constituents are pork, chicken livers and bacon, you can raid the herb garden with impunity to flavour and colour this useful cold starter or simple dish for a summer lunch. It goes down very well either with toast or hunks of French bread and the obligatory glass of chilled white wine.

450 g belly pork, minced
200 g unsmoked streaky
  bacon, minced
100 g chicken livers, finely
  chopped
3 shallots, finely chopped
2 cloves garlic, crushed
100 g sorrel leaves, washed
  and chopped
200 g spinach leaves

50 g parsley, chopped
50 g mixed fresh herbs,
  chopped fine (I use
  lovage, tarragon, chervil,
  marjoram, sage and
  thyme)
6 juniper berries, crushed
sea salt, black pepper
a beaten egg
juice of ½ lemon

1   Combine the meats in a blender and whizz briefly. Add the chopped shallots and crushed garlic plus the crushed

juniper berries. Season to taste with black pepper and salt. Whizz briefly again.

2   Place spinach and sorrel leaves in a steamer and cook for a minute or two, then transfer the cooked-down leaves to a colander and press out as much moisture as possible. Stir the spinach etc. into the mixture in the blender, and whizz until evenly distributed. Chop the herbs and parsley finely together, and add these to the blender ingredients also, together with a beaten egg and the lemon juice. Give the mixture a final whizz.

3   Turn into a pâté mould or a tin baking mould and cover either with a lid or with kitchen foil. Place the container in a roasting dish, and pour in sufficient boiling water to come halfway up the sides.

4   Cook in a moderate oven (gas 4/350 F/180 C) for 1 hour 20 minutes.

5   When done, remove the baking mould to a cool place. The terrine will have come away from the sides of the tin. Allow to cool down well, and then place a weight on top and leave until completely cold. Refrigerate overnight if possible to allow the flavours to develop.

6   Serve with hunks of fresh French bread, with perhaps some cornichons or gherkins alongside, plus a glass of summer-weight white or rosé wine!

Terrine legère
au Riesling d'Alsace

A light poultry-based terrine, ideal for a summer lunch. Be aware that this needs to be prepared a couple of days in advance!

Serves 10–12

500 g skinless chicken (or turkey) breast
500 g fillet of pork
1 garlic clove, crushed
3 shallots, chopped finely
1 medium carrot, grated coarsely
freshly ground nutmeg (or a pinch of *quatre épices Alsacien* – see page 123)

½ bottle Alsace Riesling
plenty of chopped fresh chives, parsley, chervil
150 g pure pork sausage meat
salt, pepper
bouquet garni
thin rashers of streaky bacon for lining terrine

1   The day beforehand: chop the chicken breasts and pork fillet very finely. Put the meat in a large bowl with the garlic, shallot, carrot, spice and salt and pepper to taste.

Add the wine, mix well, cover the bowl and chill for a maximum 24 hours.

2 The following day, lift the meats out of the marinade with a slotted spoon, and reserve the marinade. Mix the fresh herbs into the sausage meat and season to taste.

3 Lay the bouquet garni across the bottom of a terrine or a loaf tin. Line the tin with the bacon rashers, keeping some back for the top.

4 Layer the marinated meats with the herbed sausage meat, pouring on the reserved marinade. Finish with the remaining bacon slices.

5 Cover the terrine or tin with a double layer of foil plus a lid and put into a deep-sided roasting tin. Add water to come up to about ½ inch below the level of the top of the terrine.

6 Allow the water to come to a simmer on the top of the oven, and then carefully transfer the tin to an oven at gas 4/350 F/180 C and bake for about 1½ to 2 hours.

7 Leave the terrine to cool, weight it to compress it, and chill it until required.

Wine:
Alsace Grand Cru Riesling or a Tokay Pinot Gris.

Note:
Excellent with the following recipe as a garnish.

Spiced pears

An accompaniment to light poultry, rabbit or duck terrines.

4 ripe pears, peeled and
cored
250 g sugar
3 tsp mixed spice

2 tsp coriander seeds
grated zest and juice of
2 lemons
600 ml (1 pint) water

1   Put all the ingredients other than the pears into a pan,
    bring to the boil and then allow to simmer gently for 5
    minutes.

2   Add the pears, bring the mixture to the boil again and
    then allow to simmer until the pears are tender.*

3   Allow the pears to cool completely in the syrup –
    overnight for preference, to allow the flavours to
    permeate thoroughly. Slice as required and use to
    accompany terrines or pâtés as above.

---

* The time taken will depend on the ripeness of the pears, but properly
ripe ones should only take between 3 and 6 minutes. In the case of
under-ripe fruit the advice has to be 'until done'.

Suggestion:

This spiced pear recipe is as adaptable to savoury dishes as to sweet. Try a cinnamon or clove ice cream (see page 194) alongside... or even a gently herbal basil ice cream (page 197).

Duck à l'orange pâté

Having enjoyed its heyday back in the 1970s or thereabouts this may seem a bit of a clichéd dish these days! My own version of this retro favourite still struts its stuff, and friends don't criticise me too harshly for putting it out.

Either a 1.75 kg duck or 6 duck legs (don't be silly – ducks only have two!)
3 tbsp Armagnac brandy
125 g smoked streaky bacon
125 g onion, chopped
500 g minced pork
50 g dry white breadcrumbs
1 fat clove of garlic, chopped fine
zest of 1 orange
leaves from two sprigs of fresh thyme
½ tsp *quatre épices* (see page 123) or grated nutmeg

1 tsp sea salt
grinding of black pepper

for the stock:
bones from the duck legs, oven browned
150 ml fresh orange juice
300 ml dry white wine
600 ml water
single stick of celery, roughly chopped
a small onion, sliced
1 bay leaf
a few flat-leaf parsley stalks, lightly crushed
8 black peppercorns

1 Skin the duck legs, reserving the skin. Remove the meat from the duck legs and place in a dish. Reserve the bones to assist with the stock. Add the Armagnac to the duck meat and allow to marinate for around 1 hour.

2 Mince the duck with the onion and the bacon and stir in the minced pork with the breadcrumbs, garlic, orange zest, thyme, spice and seasonings.

3 Put all the stock ingredients into a large saucepan, having first browned the duck bones in the oven. Allow to simmer very gently for around 1 hour. Strain the stock and reduce it in a separate pan over high heat until you have around 250 ml.

4 Put the minced duck mixture into a suitable pâté dish and add the reduced stock. Put the container into a bain-marie and transfer to an oven at gas 3/325 F/170 C for around 1 hour. Test to check that the juices are no longer running pink; if they are, continue to cook for another 15–30 minutes.

5 Allow to cool and refrigerate for at least 48 hours before cutting into it.

6 Serve with a watercress and fresh orange salad and good crusty bread.

Wine:
Beaujolais-Villages: Château d'Emeringes 2005.

Duck-breast salad
with a Merlot sauce

Could be a starter... could feature as a light main course. Good for a lunch.

Serves 4

4 boneless breasts of duck
a mix of salad leaves
   (try and include some
   red ones: lollo rosso,
   radicchio, oakleaf lettuce
   etc)
2 tbsp walnut oil
a few pine kernels,
   lightly toasted or briefly
   dry-fried
1 tbsp vegetable oil
1 oz unsalted butter
salt, pepper

for the dressing:
2 shallots, chopped fine
   (or use a small red
   onion)
1 glass Merlot wine –
   drink the rest with the
   dish!
short dash of red
   wine vinegar
150 ml light vegetable oil
salt, pepper

1   Prepare the dressing first. Put the chopped shallots and the red wine in a pan and cook gently until reduced by half. Add the vinegar, and reduce again until almost all the liquid has evaporated. Gently whisk in the oil, and keep the dressing warm until needed.

2   Toss the salad leaves in the walnut oil and add salt and pepper. Divide between four plates and lightly sprinkle pine kernels on top.

3   Fry the duck breasts in the vegetable oil and butter, leaving the insides still pink, and whilst still warm slice each duck breast into thin slices and arrange on top of the lettuces.

4   Pour the warm dressing over the duck and lettuces and serve straight away.

Mushrooms on pesto crostini

Not so much a recipe, more of an insultingly easy assembly job! Given the best ingredients, though, this is a surprisingly classy vegetarian starter – and a real time-saver into the bargain!

per serving:
2 or 3 large portobello mushrooms, or fresh ceps (or a mix of smaller wild and cultivated mushrooms)
butter
a toasted round of good quality fresh bread:
ciabbata, or, best of all, olive bread
2 tbsp pesto sauce (see page 35 if you feel like making your own), thinned with extra virgin olive oil
sprig of Italian flat-leaf parsley to garnish

1   First sauté your prepared mushrooms in a little butter until soft, keeping them warm until ready to serve. Meanwhile, prepare the pesto sauce by thinning it down slightly with the olive oil.

2   Toast a good thick round of bread per person, cut them in two and put them on warmed individual serving plates.

3   Put a good tablespoon of the pesto on each and place the mushrooms on the top.

4   Dribble a little more of the pesto around the toasts and garnish each plate with a sprig of Italian flat parsley.

Fresh pesto sauce

If you are not having to rush and are prepared to make your own pesto sauce which will inevitably taste better than the shop-bought jars, this is what is involved:

Serves 6

100 g fresh basil leaves
8 tbsp extra virgin olive oil
25 g pine nuts
2 cloves of garlic, lightly
 crushed

50 g freshly grated
 Parmesan cheese
50 g freshly grated
 pecorino Romano cheese
40 g softened butter
salt

1   Put the basil, the olive oil, pine nuts, garlic and salt into a blender and pulse at high speed (you will probably have to stop from time to time to scrape the sides down into the middle again).

2   Transfer the blended ingredients to a separate dish and add the grated cheeses. When evenly blended add the softened butter.

3 For the purposes of the recipe on page 33 add further oil to the pesto to give a runny consistency; otherwise, use as a dressing for all kinds of pasta.

My salsa verde

2 cloves of fresh garlic
Maldon salt
4 anchovy fillets in olive
oil, drained and chopped
fine
a large bunch of flat-leaf
parsley (stems removed)

choice of a smaller bunch
each of: wild rocket
leaves, basil leaves, sorrel
leaves
2 tbsp red wine vinegar
a squeeze of lemon juice
6 fl oz extra virgin olive oil

1 The *traditional* way with this is to use a pestle and mortar, first mashing together the garlic cloves with some salt and then adding the anchovies. The chopped green leaves are then gradually incorporated, by which time the paste will be pretty thick.

2 Pounding as you go, add the vinegar slowly to thin the mixture, and then gradually add the olive oil until you have the consistency you want. Correct seasoning and add a little lemon juice to sharpen the flavour if desired.

3 The *time-saving* method involves a food processor. Whizz the ingredients together in the order shown above, finally adding the oil in a thin steady trickle to obtain the desired thickness of the sauce.

Salsa verde is best served immediately... though it will stand a few hours chilling in the fridge if kept in a small covered bowl, when it can be brought back to room temperature.

Greek-style grilled marinated chicken fillets

A fresh, cleanly aromatic dish perfect as a starter or as a candidate for the canapé table… Double it up and serve with a crisp salad for a light lunch.

Serves 4

2 boneless chicken breasts
4 tbsp of Greek yogurt
1 tsp ground cardamom
2 tsp lime or lemon juice

½ small chilli pepper,
   seeds removed, chopped
1 tbsp flat-leaved parsley,
   chopped
salt

1   Combine all the marinade ingredients in a bowl. Slice the chicken breast into thinnish fillets (or if adapting this recipe as canapé 'bites' to be served on sticks, into 2 cm chunks). Toss them in the marinade and leave them to stand for at least 1 hour to absorb flavours.

2   Grill or fry the chicken in batches for 5–10 minutes until it is browned and crisp on the outside and cooked through (yet moist) on the inside.

As a starter, serve with a salad and perhaps some pitta bread; alternatively, for canapés, skewer each chunk with a toothpick and serve.

Leek flamiche

A classic dish that hails originally from Flanders or northern France, a creamy tart of leeks that makes a special first course or a main dish for a light lunch.

white part of 3 or 4 good-
sized leeks, chopped
finely
100 g unsalted butter
3–4 tbsp water
salt, pepper

double cream (or
whipping cream) equal
in weight to ¼ of the
cooked leeks
500 g puff pastry (I cheat
and use shop-bought)

1 Stew the chopped leeks very gently in half the butter, adding the rest a little at a time during the cooking. Moisten with the water, cover, and cook very gently until all the moisture has been absorbed. Don't let them brown. Add the cream, mix and season well. Allow to cool.

2 Roll out half the pastry thinly to cover a round 9–10 inch baking sheet. Place the cooled leek mixture in the middle, leaving a border of about 1½ inches all round. Roll out the rest of the pastry the same way and use this to cover the leek mixture. Press the pastry edges together well to

ensure a firm seal. To help the pastry to rise, feather the edges with a sharp knife prior to baking. Glaze the surface with beaten egg, then (if you like) make a trellis-work pattern with the point of a knife.

3   Put the tart into a hot oven for 10 minutes and then lower the heat and bake for another 20 minutes. Serve very hot.

Little asparagus mousses

French gastronomic festivals abound, but few can beat the asparagus festivals held from mid April until St John's Day (24 June) in Alsace. Some of the restaurants in the most celebrated asparagus-growing areas will go overboard in basing as many courses as they can on this prized vegetable. The recipe below may well be intended for the exceptional 'white' asparagus, blanched in trenches and cut at crack of dawn each day before the tips have broken through the soil. The locals regard the more familiar green asparagus as inferior; however, they are the selfsame plant and no less delicious.

Serves 8

500 g green asparagus
6 sheets of gelatine, or
  1 sachet of powdered
  gelatine
salt, pepper

250 ml (1 cup) of
  whipping cream
dressing of salad leaves,
  your choice!

1   Lightly oil 8 small ramekins with sunflower or vegetable oil (relatively unflavoured).

2   Trim the asparagus and either steam it or cook it in boiling salted water for around 20 minutes, i.e. until it is quite tender. Drain the asparagus but reserve 1 cup of the cooking liquid. Put this in a small pan and dissolve the gelatine in it.

3   Cut the tip off 8 of the asparagus spears and reserve for decoration. Put the rest of the asparagus in a blender, whizz a bit, then add the hot dissolved gelatine and whizz again until everything is as smooth as possible. For an extra-silky finish push through a sieve, then season, and then let cool.

4   Whip the cream lightly to soft peaks and fold into the cooled asparagus purée.

5   Spoon the mixture between the 8 ramekins and chill them in the fridge until set.

6   To serve, run a knife round the edge of each mousse and, holding the ramekin firmly against the centre of each serving plate, give a good shake to release the contents. Garnish discreetly with salad leaves and a small amount of a good dressing.

Soups

Soupe à l'oignon

Serves 6

6 large onions	6 slices of bread (from a
50 g butter	baguette loaf)
1 litre vegetable stock	100 g Emmental or
salt, pepper	Gruyère cheese, grated

1   Peel and slice the onions, cooking them gently with the butter in a saucepan until they are a rich golden brown. When this stage is reached and the onions have softened add the stock and allow to simmer gently for about 15 minutes. Season to taste with salt and freshly ground black pepper.

2   If serving from an ovenproof soup tureen, lay slices of bread on the bottom and ladle the soup over them. Sprinkle with grated cheese and bake in a moderate oven until the bread and cheese are a golden brown.

3   The soup may be served in individual fondue dishes, floating a slice of bread in each.

Tip:

For a less soggy (if equally yummy) result, toast each piece of bread lightly before putting it in the soup.

Some cooks add a teaspoon of sugar to the onions in the pan when they are softening to aid the caramelising process.

Rochelle Selwyn's
chicken soup

A classic. The restorative powers of this soup are legendary. Not exactly Arnold Wesker's *Chicken Soup with Barley*, but a generic form of the time-honoured 'Jewish penicillin' from a reliable and authentic source.

1 plump boiling fowl
2 large carrots
2 sticks of celery, plus
  some of its leaves
1 Spanish onion
1 leek
1 medium-size swede
2 small white turnips
1 medium-size parsnip

2 large sprigs of fresh
  flat-leaf parsley
salt, black pepper

purists/traditionalists may
  opt to add:
approx 500 g shin of beef,
  or (not for absolute
  purists perhaps) a beef
  stock cube

1   First scald the fowl with boiling water and ensure it is perfectly clean both inside and out. If you are including giblets, ensure these are properly cleaned also. Wash the

vegetables and prepare them by cutting them into fairly large chunks.

2 Place the fowl breast side down in a very large pan with all the cut vegetables, parsley, and the shin of beef (if used). Cover with cold water. Bring to the boil and skim off any scum that rises to the top. Put a lid on the pan and simmer very gently for approx 2½ hours, turning the chicken at half time to ensure even cooking.

3 When cooked, remove chicken and vegetables. Skim the fat from the remaining soup. Adjust seasoning to taste and serve.

Emilia-Romagna bean soup with cavolo nero

Italy's province of Emilia-Romagna produces hearty and characterful soups of this kind to keep out the winter chills. A dish that adapts well to the damp British climate too! If using dried beans the soup is effectively a two-day job, the beans having been soaked in lukewarm water overnight. This is my own 'take' on an original classic.

1 kg *cavolo nero* (or substitute curly kale), washed, de-'ribbed' and chopped
100 g onion, chopped
4 tbsp olive oil
4 cloves of garlic, chopped
1 litre chicken stock

salt and fresh-ground black pepper
200 g dried borlotti beans (cranberry bean)
1 beef bouillon cube
100 g Italian *salsicce* cut into smallish chunks
6 tbsp extra virgin olive oil

1 Soak the beans overnight, drain, rinse, and cook them the following day in copious fresh unsalted water at a gentle rolling boil for about 45 minutes.* Drain and reserve.

2 In a separate pan start with the chopped onion, always a base for soups from this particular region of Italy. Sweat gently in the olive oil until gently browned.

3 Add the chopped garlic, and continue to cook until it has taken on some colour.

4 Cut away the tougher 'ribs' and chop the leaves of *cavolo nero* (or curly kale) fairly finely. Rinse them, and turn them in the hot oil sufficiently to allow them to be coated thoroughly and to be cooked down just a little.

5 Pour in the chicken stock and sufficient extra water (if necessary) to cover the ingredients by about 1 inch.

6 Allow to cook gently for at least an hour to ensure the vegetables are sufficiently softened.

7 Meanwhile cut the *salsicce* into small chunks and dry-fry very briefly in a separate frying pan. Reserve. You are seeking simply to blanch it prior to adding it to the soup, not to 'frizzle' it.

8 After the basic soup ingredients have spent their hour in the pan, add the sausage, the beans, the beef bouillon cube plus sufficient water to replace what has already been lost in the pan by evaporation. Cook very gently together for a further 30 minutes.

---

* The cooking time will vary depending on how old or dry your dried beans happen to be. The rule of thumb for cooking seems to be to cover the soaked beans with unsalted fresh water allowing about 3 inches depth above them, and give them around 40–45 minutes at a gentle rolling boil. Add salt only at the point you want to incorporate them into the dish you are preparing otherwise they toughen unacceptably.

9   For service, toast a slice of country bread for each warmed soup dish and pour a little extra virgin olive oil over each slice. Ladle out the soup on top of the bread and hand round some grated Parmigiano Reggiano cheese to be sprinkled over if desired.

Turnip and brown bread soup

Cheap, warming, and with a unique taste that is more than the sum of its constituent parts, this soup appears as an historical English recipe mentioned by Michael Smith in Geraldene Holt's *Fine English Cookery*. I have included it not only because it is delicious as a winter warmer but because those eating it might have a hard time guessing its humble constituents!

75 g butter
35 g chopped shallot
500 g turnips, peeled
75 g brown bread, crusts
   removed
1 tbsp vegetable oil

750 ml chicken stock
½ tsp freshly grated
   nutmeg
salt, pepper
sprig of parsley, and
   cream, to garnish

1   In a medium-sized saucepan sweat the chopped shallots in half the butter, allowing them to brown slightly at the edges. Peel the turnips and cut into dice, add them to the shallots and stir well to coat them with the butter. Turn

down the heat, put a lid on the pan, and allow to cook very gently for about 20 minutes or until tender.

2   Cut the crusts off the bread and cut it into crouton-sized cubes. In a separate shallow pan heat the remaining butter with the oil, and sauté the bread croutons until browned nicely on all sides. Reserve.

3   When the turnip is cooked, add half the croutons, the nutmeg and the chicken stock to the turnip pan and simmer gently for a further 20 minutes. Taste to correct seasoning, then whizz in a blender to liquidise.

4   Serve with a little swirl of cream and decorate with a little chopped parsley and the remaining croutons. Hand round a good sourdough bread as an accompaniment.

Lentil and herb soup

This is an old favourite culled from *The Herb Book* by Arabella Boxer and Philippa Brack.

I have only recently tried growing lovage again, which is a good excuse to make this fragrant but homely soup.

100 g brown or red lentils
2 pints of stock: vegetable,
  chicken or veal
a small onion
1½ tbsp olive oil
1 clove garlic
100 g spinach or
  spinach beet

sea salt, black pepper
50 g mixed chopped fresh
  herbs: sorrel, parsley,
  lovage, tarragon,
  lemon thyme
juice of ½ small lemon
150 ml natural yogurt or
  buttermilk

1 In a large pan simmer the lentils in the stock, having first brought the items to the boil (a 30-minute simmer for red or 45 for brown).

2 Chop the onion and finely chop the garlic. Heat the oil in a separate pan and sauté the onion gently until soft and translucent, then add the garlic. Allow them to cook gently together for a minute or two. Reserve.

3   Once the lentils are soft, chop the spinach and add it to the pan, adding seasoning to taste. Allow the spinach to simmer through until soft (5–8 minutes), and then add the onion and garlic plus the freshly chopped herbs. Simmer together for a further 2–3 minutes and then transfer to a blender. Whizz briefly, and then add 1 tbsp lemon juice and the yogurt or buttermilk.

4   Serve immediately with good crusty bread.

Note:

5   The soup is also excellent served cold.

Fresh pea soup with slow-cooked ham hock

A close cousin to the *potage Saint-Germain* of French classic cuisine. Out of season, failing tiny fresh garden peas, frozen *petits pois* may be used, although the result may taste less delicate.

Serves 4

1 kg fresh garden peas,
  podded
3 'little gem' lettuces,
  shredded
12 tiny button onions or
  4 spring onions
a few sprigs of parsley
a few sprigs of chervil
1 litre vegetable stock
90 g butter
1 egg yolk

75 ml double cream
salt, pepper

for the dressing:
4 oz of slow-cooked ham
  hock, shredded and kept
  warm
pea shoots and
  micro-greens

1   Melt 60 g of the butter in a large heavy-bottomed saucepan and add the peas, the shredded lettuce, the chopped onions and the herbs, and 'sweat' together on a low heat for about 5 minutes until softened, stirring frequently.

2   Pour in the vegetable stock and simmer together for 25–30 minutes. Transfer to a blender when everything has softened (reserving a few whole peas for subsequent decoration) and blitz until very smooth. Return the liquid to the pan.

3   Meanwhile, combine the egg yolk and the cream in a small bowl, stir in a ladleful of the soup, and gradually add this mixture to the contents of the pan over a low heat, stirring as you go, and add salt and pepper to taste.

4   To serve, place a little mound of the pulled slow-cooked ham hock to make an 'island' in the centre of each empty warmed soup plate. Dress each ham 'island' with a few pea-shoots, tiny leaf greens and a few of the cooked reserved peas, and pour the soup around it at table.

Fish

Trota alla Veneziana

This simple Venetian way with trout has always appealed to me. The flavours are positive and distinctively Italian... sorry, Venetian – there *is* a difference!

4 cleaned trout (not too
  big)
75 g butter
4 tbsp flat-leaf parsley,
  chopped fine
8 fresh sage leaves,
  chopped fine

white wine, sufficient to
  cover
salt, pepper
small tot of grappa (or
  brandy)

1. Make a stuffing combining the herbs, butter and seasonings. Pack it equally into the cleaned stomach cavity of each fish, enclosing it using a toothpick.
2. Place the fish on a suitable baking dish, pour sufficient wine over to cover and cook in a moderate oven for about 15 minutes – or until the fish is cooked through.
3. Finally, heat a little grappa or brandy in a spoon, set it alight and pour over the cooked fish.
4. Serve with new potatoes and fresh spinach cooked with a good knob of butter.

Wine:
A crisp, northern Italian white: lightly spicy Tocai Friulano or a Pinot Bianco.

Gravadlax 'Black Watch'

A Scandinavian recipe for cured raw salmon remembered from my first cruise with Fred. Olsen lines as a guest food/wine lecturer. 'Graveyard' salmon or 'buried' salmon is not the most attractive of translations from the Norwegian, but it is a real winner for a big buffet party – folks really do come back for more. Farmed salmon, although less expensive, is hardly comparable in flavour and texture to wild; however, given the treatment required here, the cheaper version is perfectly adequate for this dish.

Don't skimp on time: a five-day cure is probably about right.

Ask your fishmonger to cut the salmon into two big flank fillets, leaving the skin on.

Serves 16–20

1 farmed salmon weighing
  2.25–3.25 kg (5–7 lbs)
4 tbsp demerara sugar
2 tbsp Maldon salt
1 bunch fresh dill, stalks
  removed, chopped

2 tsp crushed black
  peppercorns
Norwegian aquavit (or
  brandy) to moisten.

1. Put one fillet skin side down on an oiled sheet of kitchen foil – the biggest size.

2. Make the 'cure' mixture of sugar, salt and pepper, and spread this evenly over the flesh side of the fillet; sprinkle chopped fresh dill over the fish and moisten with a slosh of aquavit. Put the other fillet on top to form a kind of sandwich.

3. Wrap the salmon securely in *two* layers of foil and put it in a suitable lipped dish in the refrigerator, placing a weighted board on top to compress the fish.

4. Turn the package over daily, replacing the weighted board. The package is likely to exude a little sugary/salty fluid, so make sure this doesn't reach other items in the fridge unless you want to 'cure' them as well! (NB: Fresh milk kept in the fridge during the curing process tends to turn sour fairly quickly!)

5. At the end of the five days, remove the package from the fridge and gently wash excess curing juices from the surface of the gravadlax. Remove any remaining pin bones with tweezers, if necessary.

6. Slice fairly thinly – though not as thinly as you would for smoked salmon – and serve with a mustard and dill sauce (see next page).

7. Have some Scandinavian black bread or rye bread to hand.

Wine?

No. Chilled aquavit, genever gin or schnapps? Yes!

Mustard and dill sauce

The perfect accompaniment to the gravadlax recipe above.

bunch of fresh dill
3 tbsp Dijon or German
  mustard

100 ml olive oil
100 ml whipping cream
salt, pepper

1   Whizz all the ingredients except the cream in a blender
    until emulsified, then add the cream and give a brief final
    whizz. Check seasoning.

Scallops with lentils and coriander

The sweetness of scallops is set off here by an intriguingly aromatic lentil sauce – the coriander element giving a hint of Thai influence, perhaps.

Serves 4–6

16 large fresh scallops with corals
2 tbsp sunflower oil
50 g large brown lentils (or use Puy lentils)
1 crushed clove of garlic
small onion, chopped fine
1-inch piece of fresh root ginger, chopped fine
1 tsp cardamom seeds, ground

2 tbsp Italian tomato *passata*, or two ripe tomatoes seeded, skinned and chopped
250 ml chicken stock
50 g unsalted butter
small bunch of fresh coriander, leaves chopped
squeeze of lemon juice
salt, pepper

1   Thoroughly clean the scallops and slice the flesh transversally into three. Reserve the pink roes.

2   Season well. Pour a little sunflower oil into a bowl or a plastic food-wrapper bag and coat the scallops in the oil. Reserve.

3   Rinse the lentils well and parboil them for about 20 minutes, or until just tender. Drain and reserve.

4   In the remaining oil, gently fry the onion, garlic and ginger until golden. Add crushed cardamom seeds and the *passata* or prepared tomatoes and cook for a further minute. Remove from the heat. Add all the stock to the pan with half the reserved lentils. Simmer gently for about 15 minutes and then whizz in a blender to liquidise.

5   Return the liquidised sauce to the pan and add the remaining lentils and the fresh chopped coriander leaves. Reheat gently.

6   Meanwhile heat a dry frying pan, add the reserved scallops and roes and fry very quickly on both sides... just sufficiently for them to lose their raw colour.

7   Spoon the sauce equally into warmed serving bowls and mount the cooked scallops on top.

8   Decorate each bowl with a sprig of coriander.

Wine:
Something to echo the sweetness of the fish and gentle spices of the sauce: a voluptuous oaked Chardonnay from South Australia... or Santa Julia Viognier from Argentina.

Sea bass on a bed of caramelised red cabbage

Serves 4

4 thick portions of sea
  bass, skin left on
1 red cabbage, shredded
75 g (3 oz) unsalted butter
½ pint red wine
a good splosh of *crème de
  cassis*
¼ pint of chicken stock
salt, pepper

for the sauce:
½ pint fish stock
¼ pint dry white wine
¼ pint vermouth (ideally
  Noilly Prat)
¼ pint chicken stock
1 clove garlic, crushed
1 small shallot, chopped
  fine
½ pint double cream

1 Slash each portion of fish three times across the skin.
2 Put the shredded cabbage in a saucepan with an ounce of
   butter and add the wine, the *cassis* and the chicken stock.
   Bring up to a boil and then allow to simmer and reduce
   very gently for 45 minutes, by which time the cabbage
   should have caramelised. Stir occasionally and, having
   checked for seasoning, keep gently warmed ready for use.

3   Put all the sauce ingredients except the cream in a pan and reduce by fast boiling to about two thirds of the original volume. Add the cream and reduce again until the sauce is thick enough to coat the back of a spoon. Remove from the heat and pass through a sieve.

4   Heat the remaining butter in a pan until hot and seal the fish on the flesh side. Turn it over and cook on the skin side for about 8–10 minutes over a medium heat until crisp.

5   To serve, divide the cabbage between four plates, lay the fish skin side upwards on top, and pour the sauce around it.

Wine:
Alsace Pinot Gris.

Hot-smoked salmon fillets with chervil butter sauce and garnish of quail egg tart

This is a recipe involving several separate elements. It is time-consuming to prepare, certainly, but the results seem to justify the trouble taken.

Serves 4

4 quail eggs
4 oz puff pastry
4 smoked salmon fillets
salt, pepper

for the mushroom purée:
2 shallots, finely chopped
1 oz unsalted butter
7 oz small chestnut
 mushrooms
7 fl oz red wine
a dollop of double cream

for the sauce:
3 shallots, finely chopped
¼ pint dry white wine
a dash of white wine
 vinegar
1 dollop of double cream
12 oz of unsalted butter
salt, pepper
a bunch of chervil,
 chopped finely

1 Initially prepare the quail eggs. They should be boiled for no longer than 2½ minutes in rapidly boiling water. Cool them rapidly under a cold tap and peel them. Place them in a bowl, covered by cold water, and put into the fridge until required.

2 Roll out the puff pastry until *very* thin and line four 1½-inch tartlet cases. Transfer these to the fridge and allow to chill for an hour. Remove from the fridge and bake 'blind' in an oven at gas 4/350 F/180 C for 10 minutes.

3 Sweat the chopped shallots in butter until softened and translucent, then transfer them to a food processor and blitz them briefly with the mushrooms. Add this mixture to a dry, heavy frying pan, add the wine, and allow to cook slowly until the liquid has evaporated.

4 To prepare the salmon, pin-bone the fillets if necessary and cut each piece into diagonal ¼-inch slices. Overlap each three-slice portion on buttered kitchen foil.

5 For the sauce: In a small pan reduce the shallots, wine and vinegar until almost dry! Add the cream. Bring to the boil, then over a low heat whisk in the butter, cut into small pieces. Add most of the chopped chervil to the sauce, reserving some for a garnish. Keep the sauce warm...

6 Finishing off: Warm the mushroom purée into which you have stirred the reserved cream. Warm the tarts. Warm the salmon by steaming it for a couple of minutes, adding the eggs to the steam-cooking for the last 30 seconds.

7 Put a pastry tart on each plate, fill the bottom with the mushroom purée and rest an egg on top of each. Arrange three salmon slices on each plate, fanning them out to look attractive. Pour the sauce around, and garnish with the remaining chervil.

Wine:
The smoked fish calls for a softly aromatic wine like a dry Muscat or a Viognier.

Paella Valenciana

This is a coastal variation of the generic Spanish *paella*. Inland versions may include rabbit, spicy sausage or even game. Local oranges and soft fruits aside, Valencia is also the biggest rice-growing area in the western world!

Serves 4

4 tbsp olive oil
2 lb chicken pieces
2 Spanish onions, chopped
4 cloves garlic, crushed
1 tbsp paprika
350 g risotto rice
2 large *marmande* tomatoes, peeled, seeded and chopped
1.75 litres hot chicken stock
1 finger-length sprig of rosemary

large pinch saffron threads, pounded
225 g small squid, cleaned and cut up
150 g green beans
500 g mussels in their shells
225 g raw prawns or langoustines in their shells
115 g broad beans
salt, pepper

1   Heat the oil in a wide shallow casserole pan (or a *paella* pan if you happen to have one). Add the pieces of chicken and cook until lightly browned (10–12 minutes). Add the onion and the garlic and fry for five minutes until softened.

2   Add the paprika and then the rice. Stir until well mixed together and then pour in the hot chicken stock, the tomato, the rosemary and the seasonings of salt and pepper.

3   Dissolve the pounded saffron in 2 tablespoons of the stock (or white wine), add it to the mixture in the pan and cook everything together at a brisk temperature for about 10 minutes.

4   Prepare the squid, cleaning carefully under running water. Reserve the bodies and the tentacles. Cut the body sacs into rings and chop the tentacles. Cut the green beans into lengths. Scatter all the seafood, the green beans and the broad beans into the *paella*. *Do not stir.*

5   Turn down the heat and simmer gently for 8–10 minutes until the liquid has been absorbed by the rice. Cover the pan, allowing the seafood and beans to steam gently in the heat from the *paella* beneath.

6   Remove from the heat, allow to rest a minute or two, and serve.

Wine:

Call me old-fashioned, but a traditional white Rioja, Marques de Murrieta Reserva, with its oaky, slightly oxidised character, would be a perfectly idiomatic accompaniment.

Warm crab and fresh tarragon tart

This combination of flavours really works!

for the pastry:
200 g plain flour
175 g butter (cold, cut into
  chunks)
1 egg yolk
2 tbsp ice-cold water

for the filling:
500 g crab
3 eggs
300 ml double cream
2 tsp French mustard
1 heaped tbsp fresh
  tarragon leaves (about
  30–40 leaves)
2 tbsp grated Parmesan
  cheese

1 First make the pastry and set it aside to chill and rest for
   about an hour.
2 Roll out the pastry thinly and use to line a buttered 24 cm
   tart tin. Prick the bottom with a fork, put a lining of
   baking foil on top of the pastry and add either ceramic
   baking 'beans' or dried beans as a weight to keep the foil

in place. Chill again for 15 minutes, then bake 'blind' for a further 15 minutes. Allow to cool.

3   For the filling: separate the eggs. In a bowl, mix the yolks with the cream, add salt, pepper and the French mustard, then chop and add the tarragon and the crab meat. Stir gently to combine. In a separate bowl beat the egg whites into stiff peaks and then fold them gently into the crab custard using a metal spatula or spoon.

4   Pour the mixture into the pastry case and finish with a sprinkle of Parmesan cheese.

5   Bake the tart in a gas 5/375 F/190 C oven for 25–30 minutes. When cooked to perfection, the centre should still be slightly wobbly. Allow to cool.

6   Serve warm with an accompaniment of watercress or salad leaves.

Wine:

Either a Clare Valley Riesling from South Australia, or Jackson Estate Sauvignon Blanc (Marlborough NZ).

Monkfish in spiced yogurt sauce

This taste-laden recipe benefits from a little advance preparation involving the fish being bathed in a marinade for about 2 hours before cooking.

monkfish, a good piece
1 aubergine
extra virgin olive oil
½ a can of chopped
    tomatoes
large carton of Greek-style
    yogurt

2 green chillies
fresh dill or fennel
fresh parsley or coriander
lemon juice
salt, pepper

1   First prepare the aubergine, slice it in thin rounds, salt them, rinse and pat them dry with kitchen towel, then fry lightly in the oil, removing excess oil on kitchen towel.
2   Peel half the slices and whizz in a blender with the yogurt, the tomatoes, the chillies and herbs until smooth. Season with lemon juice, salt and pepper to taste.
3   Marinate the fish in the sauce for about 2 hours, then put the aubergine slices into the bottom of an ovenproof dish

and add the fish and the sauce. Put a cover on the dish, or cover with foil, and put in a moderate oven for around 45 minutes.

4   Serve with the sauce and plainly boiled or steamed rice.

A crisp beer batter
for fried fish

My own versions of batter for fried fish had always included egg, which in my opinion can give rather soft or flabby results; so I was more than delighted to find this invaluable recipe from Galton Blackiston's *Summertime* cookbook which, for me at least, is 'the business'.

125 g plain flour
½ tsp baking powder
½ tsp bicarbonate of soda
50 g cornflour

½ tsp ground coriander
  (optional)
½ tsp ground cumin
225 ml chilled lager beer
salt, pepper

1   Mix all dry ingredients well together in a bowl, and keep by until you want to make the batter. When ready, add the lager all at once and stir in quickly... avoid lumps if you can.

2   Put some seasoned flour on a plate and coat the pieces of fish in it, shaking off the excess before dunking each piece into the batter mix.

3   Fry lightly in vegetable oil at a cooking temperature of around 300 F/140–160 C.

Meat dishes

Traditional steak and kidney pie

My father always referred to this favourite dish as 'Kate and Sidney'. In Victorian times, poorer households bulked out the relatively expensive steak both with kidneys and oysters... the latter being cheap in those days.

There are various recipes for this British classic. Here, the flavours truly 'sing' and in my opinion put a famous London restaurant's version firmly in the shade!

Serves 4–6

454 g ox or lamb's kidneys, cored
900 g blade steak (chuck)
100 g plain flour seasoned liberally with salt and pepper
corn or vegetable oil
4 medium onions

600 ml beef stock (see footnote on next page)
½ tsp ground cloves
1 tbsp chopped parsley
1 tbsp chopped fresh marjoram
1 bay leaf
puff pastry for lid
egg wash

1   First prepare the kidneys, core them and cut them into smallish pieces. Soak them in water for an hour, or overnight in the refrigerator. Rinse through, drain and pat them dry.

2   Trim the steak and cut it into bitesize pieces. Roll in seasoned flour, shaking off any excess. Heat the oil in a frying pan and brown the steak pieces on all sides. (Don't overcrowd the pan. Cook the steak in batches, stirring the meat round from time to time to ensure all sides are cooked.) Once browned, transfer the meat to a casserole.

3   Slice the onions and fry them until they've taken colour – you may need to use a little more oil. Transfer them to the casserole once cooked.

4   Lightly fry the kidneys in the same pan, just sufficiently to firm them up and lose their pink colour. Transfer them to the casserole.

5   Add the prepared beef stock,* the fresh chopped herbs and the ground cloves. Give the ingredients a good stir.

6   Cook for 1 hour at gas 5/375 F/190 C, remove from the oven and stir again. Replace in the oven and cook for a further 45 minutes to an hour, or until the meat is perfectly tender.

7   Remove casserole from the oven, cool and, if necessary, skim off any excess fat. Transfer the contents to a pie dish.

8   Roll out the puff pastry; I admit I use shop-bought stuff on occasion – good enough, and saves time.

---

* A beef bouillon cube makes only a fair standby. A classic beef stock involving a reduction of rib bones of beef, vegetables and herbs had not recently been possible for domestic cooks in the UK until beef 'on the bone' was brought back into circulation. So if you have both the bones and the time...

9   Cut inch-wide strips to go round the rim of the pie dish, using egg wash as 'glue', and then paint egg wash on top of the strips to act as 'glue' for the pastry canopy. Put a pie funnel in the middle of the dish to act as a ventilator, add the casserole contents and put the pastry lid over the top, pressing down the edges to ensure a good seal. Decorate with 'leaves' made of pastry trimmings, and paint with egg wash again.

10 Transfer to the oven at gas 6/400 F/200 C and cook until the pastry top is well browned… about 15–20 minutes.

Rushed? Try this:

If I'm pushed for time I admit to taking a short cut. I omit the pie-dish stage altogether and make the pie-crust top separately: I roll out a 12-inch pastry disk onto a baking sheet, decorate with 'leaves' and egg-wash glaze as before, and cook it at gas 6/400 F/200 C for 15 minutes or so. Add a slice of crust to each serving from the casserole. It is a pity for guests not to see the pie in all its glory, but even if served as above the tastes are no less scrummy!

Boiled or steamed parsleyed potatoes and broccoli seem appropriate vegetables.

Wine:

Reds of ripe fruit and intensity: Merlot or Cabernet/Shiraz from Coonawarra, Australia; or Rutherford Ranch Zinfandel, Napa, California.

Medallions de porc
à la Dijonnaise

When a dish is cooked *à la Dijonnaise* it is usually understood that mustard is involved somewhere in the process. This simple Burgundian dish is no exception, as a touch of the local mustard lends piquancy to a rich cream sauce. The inclusion of sliced pickled gherkins or cornichons adds its own acetic touch to set the other flavours off perfectly.

Serves 4

2 tenderloins of pork, sliced into ½-inch rounds
25 g butter
2 tbsp vegetable oil

for the sauce:
500 ml heavy cream
4 pickled gherkins, sliced
1 tbsp shallots, chopped fine
1 tbsp Dijon mustard
short dash of white wine vinegar
salt, pepper

1. First assemble the sauce ingredients – the cream, the chopped gherkins, shallots, the mustard, the vinegar and seasonings – in a small bowl and stir to combine.

2. Heat a frying pan, add butter and oil and gently fry the 'medallions' of pork until browned on both sides.

3. Add the prepared sauce, let it bubble for a minute and then cook on a reduced heat for a couple of minutes while the pork cooks through, stirring the pan contents occasionally to prevent any burning.

4. Serve up with French fries or sautéed potatoes or, better, Lyonnaise potatoes, plus a green vegetable like Kenya beans… or simply a crisp green salad.

Wine:
A simple red Burgundy is ideal here.

Raised pork pie

A labour of love, but worth it! Traditional raised pies need a good savoury jelly, which should be prepared first – even a day ahead. NB: You will need a pie tin with hinged or clipped sides which can be removed easily when the pie is cooked.

Serves 8–10

for the jelly:
2 pigs' trotters, split
bones from pork
veal knuckle
large carrot, sliced
large onion stuck with
    4 cloves
12 peppercorns

for the pie crust:
1 kg plain flour
500 ml water (approx)
250 g lard
1 tsp salt
2 tbsp icing sugar
beaten egg (for glaze)

for the pie filling:
1 kg of boned pork
    shoulder (fatty if
    possible) – or use fat end
    of belly pork
225 g of finely chopped
    unsmoked bacon rashers
small bunch of fresh sage,
    finely chopped
½ tsp each of powdered
    clove, nutmeg, allspice
a tsp of anchovy essence
    (optional)

1   Put all the jelly ingredients into a large pan. Fill with water to cover generously and simmer gently for about 3 hours. *Do not add salt.*

2   Strain the stock into a clean pan and boil the quantity down vigorously to about 1 pint.

3   Add seasonings of salt and plenty of pepper, and leave to cool.

4   To make the crust: sift the flour, salt and sugar into a bowl. In a separate pan bring the water and lard to a boil and, once boiling, pour it onto the ingredients already in the bowl, stirring with a wooden spoon until a smooth dough is obtained. This will be hot! Allow to cool a little and reserve about a quarter of the mixture to make a pie lid plus any decorations (keep it somewhere warm!). Meanwhile, line the interior of the *greased* pie tin with the warm malleable pastry, ensuring there are no holes through which any pie juices could escape. Build the pastry up from the bottom to the top of the sides.

5   Make the filling: chop the pork finely, or mince it fairly coarsely. Chop *half* of the bacon finely, reserving the remaining rashers to line the interior of the pie. Combine the rest of the bacon, chopped, with the pork and add the sage, spices and anchovy essence to the mixture. Blend well.

6   Fill the pie crust with the filling, ensuring that it is mounded up sufficiently to support the lid. Brush the top edges of the pastry with beaten egg as a 'glue', and roll out the remaining pastry to cover the top. Cut 'leaves' or 'roses' from any leftover pastry to decorate the top, make a good ventilation hole in the centre, and brush the entire lid surface with beaten egg as a glaze.

7   Bake for 30 minutes at gas 6/400 F/200 C, then reduce the heat and continue to cook for 1½ hours at gas 3/325 F/ 170 C.

8   Remove the pie from the oven. Let it cool down a little. Remove the hinged metal pastry case and brush the sides of the cooked pie with beaten egg. Return it to the oven for about ten minutes to allow the sides to take colour; meanwhile, don't forget to cover the top of the pie with foil or greaseproof paper to prevent it from burning.

9   Remove the pie from the oven once again and add the cooled reserved jelly – in a just-runny state – through the hole in the top of the pastry via a funnel.

10 Cool, chill in a refrigerator, and serve the next day having allowed the flavours to develop.

Classic beef gulyas with caraway dumplings

Of the many recipes I have attempted for *gulyas*, or 'goulash', this one seems to be the most authentic. Would it be recognised as the real thing both in Hungary, Austria and the Czech Republic? I hope so. The best part about it is that once the initial work is done the dish looks after itself... and the slow-cook aromas are decidedly tempting.

Serves 4

1 kg blade steak (chuck),
   cut into bitesize cubes
750 g onions, chopped
1½ tbsp mild paprika
1½ tbsp concentrated
   tomato paste
1 pinch of hot chilli
   powder
1 tsp caraway seeds
   (optional)
150 ml vegetable oil

2 tsp vinegar
a sprig of fresh marjoram
   (or 1 tsp dried)
200 ml water or stock

for the caraway dumplings:
125 g self-raising flour
65 g shredded beef suet
1 tsp caraway seeds
salt

1   In a heatproof casserole big enough to hold all the ingredients, first fry the onions in oil until they turn golden. Then add the paprika, the pinch of chilli powder and the teaspoon of caraway seeds (if using them). Stir until well combined and remove to a warm plate.

2   Put a little more oil into the original pan and add the cubed steak. Once browned on all sides return the onion/paprika, combine well with the meat, cover and allow to simmer very gently for about 5 minutes.

3   Add the stock or water, the tomato purée, the vinegar, marjoram and salt.

4   Stir everything together, cover the casserole and cook over the gentlest heat for about 3 hours. Alternatively put the casserole into a very low oven, gas 1/275 F/140 C.

5   To make the dumplings: first, dry-fry the caraway seeds in a small pan for a minute and reserve. Sift the flour into a bowl, mix in the shredded suet, the caraway seeds and some salt, and add just sufficient cold water to make a firm pastry. Make walnut-sized balls of the pastry, and cook in simmering water for about 15 minutes. (Don't let the water boil rapidly as the dumpling balls will break up.)

6   Serve the *gulyas* with the caraway dumplings and either plainly boiled potatoes or noodles. If serving at a dinner party you could top the *gulyas* with flat egg noodles, cooked until tender, covered with 100 g cottage cheese and pieces of hot crispy bacon… topped off with a *gremolata* of chopped parsley combined with freshly grated lemon peel.

Wine:

For *gulyas*, ideally a soft, spicy Hungarian red like Bull's Blood (Egri Bikaver) or Kadarka. Alternatively – a heresy – a heavyweight white Burgundy, e.g. a Meursault!

Leftovers?
Thin down with a little good beef stock, whizz in a blender, add a touch of sour cream, reheat, adjust seasoning... and there's a winter-warming *gulasch-suppe.*

Stracotto al Barolo

Various recipes exist for this classic Piemontese dish, although the most authentic I have found is as follows, which requires at least 24 hours' preliminary preparation.

Serves 6

1 kg braising beef in one piece
2 carrots, chopped
1 medium onion, coarsely chopped
2 celery stalks, chopped roughly
½ cup of flat-leaf parsley, chopped fine

2 bay leaves
1 tbsp juniper berries
1 tsp black peppercorns
½ cup lard, diced
½ bottle Barolo wine
butter, olive oil
salt

1   The day before you plan to serve the dish, put the meat, the chopped vegetables and the herbs into a bowl. Pour the wine over and marinate in a cool place for at least 24 hours.

2   Take the meat out of the marinade, which should be reserved. Dry it well with paper towels and brown the

meat thoroughly on all sides in a heatproof casserole in the butter and oil. Using a slotted spoon, transfer the chopped vegetables to join the meat. Add a cupful of the marinade wine and salt and pepper to taste. Cover the casserole and braise in a low oven (gas 4/350 F/180 C) for 3–4 hours. Keep an eye on the levels of liquid in the casserole and add more of the marinade as seems necessary to prevent the meat from drying out.

3   When the dish is done, remove the meat to a warmed platter. Pour the sauce with its vegetables into a food processor and whizz to a textured purée, reheat, and pour over the meat.

4   Serve with polenta or potatoes.

Wine:

Barolo DOCG, or another Nebbiolo-based wine such as Spanna or Chiavennasca.

Braised pork with bay leaves

This simple dish, *maiale all'alloro,* is a southern Italian classic, redolent of aromatic herbs. Ideally suited to loin of pork, it adapts well to other cuts.

Serves 4–6

2 tbsp extra virgin olive oil
1 loin of pork weighing
  around 1 kg (2.2lb)
1 tbsp juniper berries,
  crushed
2 cloves

3 medium-sized bay leaves
2 medium onions,
  chopped
salt, pepper
8 fl oz dry white wine

1. In a casserole or pan just large enough to hold the meat, heat the oil until a faint haze arises from it.

2. Add the pork and brown it gently on all sides for about 10 minutes.

3. Add the juniper berries, cloves, bay leaves and onions, plus a seasoning of salt and a few good grinds of black pepper.

4   Lower the heat under the pan and cook very slowly for around 1½–2 hours, moistening the meat with a little of the wine from time to time (use around ½ cup).

5   Slice the meat and arrange on a serving dish. Keep it warm. Meanwhile add the remaining wine to the pan residues and bring to the boil, scraping up any browned bits. Run this little sauce through a sieve and pour over the meat. Serve up at once.

Wine:
Aglianico di Vulture.

Saucisson de Toulouse

The classic recipe from the Languedoc owes as much to the simplicity of its preparation as to the unique quality of the back fat of the local pork which, chopped fairly coarsely, keeps the sausages moist. If you have a friendly local butcher he may be happy to order you a salted hank of hog casings which you'll need for the sausage skins.

Makes 10 sausages

600 g lean pork
200 g pork fat
1 small clove of garlic,
   chopped fine
1 tbsp chopped parsley
1 heaped tsp of rock salt
   and black peppercorns
   crushed together
pinch *quatre épices* (see
   page 123), or grated
   nutmeg

2 oz sausage casings (well
   soaked in water)

equipment:
sausage-stuffing tube (the
   manual variety may give
   greater control than the
   machine-driven kind)
fine-gauge kitchen string

1   Work both the lean and the fat pork through the coarse plate of a mincer or grinder, add the spice and seasonings and chill well (overnight if possible) to let the flavours infuse. When chilled and rested, test for seasoning by sautéing a small piece of the mixture. Correct seasoning to taste if necessary.

2   Making up: Soak the sausage casings in cold water for about an hour. These generally come packed in salt, so they'll need a thorough rinse through in clean water before use. For convenience use about 24 inches of casing at a time. Tie a knot in one end of the casing and attach the open end to the delivery end of a sausage stuffer, pushing the casing onto its tube until the tied end is reached. Work the filling through the tube, letting the empty skins take up the mixture. Take care not to overfill the sausages as you go. Either tie each 'link' with fine kitchen string or simply twist the sausage skins to make individual 4- to 6-inch links as you fill them up. Finally prick the skins with a pin where any air pockets show.

3   Grill or broil the sausages, having brushed them with melted butter beforehand.

Sausage variations:
You could omit the garlic or add different herbs, or blend chopped diced apple into the basic mix or use pistachio nuts etc. etc. The world is your sausage! At home I usually derind and bone out a hand (spring) of pork plus about 500 g of the fatter end of pork belly to provide sufficient balance between fat and lean meat.

Sauté d'agneau
à la Navarraise

A classic recipe not, as the name suggests, from the Spanish side of the Pyrenees but from the French, marrying sweet peppers with lamb. It recalls the days when the ancient Kingdom of Navarre stretched as far northwards as Bordeaux.

Serves 6

1 leg of lamb, boned, and
  cut into 2 cm cubes
salt, pepper
60 g unsalted butter
5 tbsp olive oil
2 onions, peeled and thinly
  sliced

6 sweet red capsicums,
  seeded and broadly diced
1 clove garlic, crushed
1 tbsp vinegar
1 tsp paprika
dash of cayenne pepper, or
  a dash of Tabasco
parsley, to garnish

1 Season the cubed lamb with salt and pepper. Heat 2 tbsp of the oil with the butter in a large heavy frying pan, and sauté the lamb until golden brown at the edges.

2 Stir in the sliced onions and cover the pan. Cook, stirring, for 5 minutes. Stir in the vinegar then remove the pan, still covered, from the heat.

3 In a second frying pan gently sauté the diced red peppers, stirring well. Stir in the garlic and paprika and cook gently for 7 or 8 minutes.

4 Add the peppers to the meat, then stir in the cayenne. Check seasoning.

5 Simmer very gently, uncovered, for a further 5 minutes.

6 Transfer to a warmed serving dish. Sprinkle with parsley and serve.

Wine:
Ochoa Navarra Reserva, for preference, or try a Tempranillo from Valdepeñas.

Abbacchio alla cacciatora 'Trastevere'

This robustly flavoured braised lamb dish hails originally from the bustling area across the Tiber from central Rome, home to many good local *trattorie*.

Serves 6

3 tbsp good olive oil
4 flat anchovy fillets in oil, drained and chopped
1 tsp crushed dried red peppers
1 kg cubed lamb (choose either leg, shoulder or neck)
salt, pepper

300 ml dry white wine
short dash of good red wine vinegar
3 or 4 cloves of garlic, chopped finely
1 tsp dried oregano
1 tsp '00' superfine plain flour
parsley, for decoration

1   In a heavy casserole (with a lid) combine the oil and the crumbled dried red pepper. Cook together over a gentle heat for about 5 minutes.

2　Meanwhile cut the lamb into cubes. Raise the heat under the pan and brown the lamb pieces for 5 minutes or so, taking care not to crowd the pan. (Cook in batches if need be.) Season the meat and then add the wine, the vinegar and the chopped garlic.

3　Reduce the heat to low, and allow to cook for about an hour until everything is tender. At this point, remove the lamb from the casserole juices and keep the pieces warm in a low oven.

4　In a separate pan combine the oregano, the chopped anchovy fillets and the flour (or use cornflour) with a few tablespoonfuls of the casserole juices to moisten, and cook very gently, stirring for a minute or two until the mixture has thickened. Whisk this back into the juices remaining in the main pan.

5　Serve the lamb on warmed plates, spooning the sauce over, and then decorate each dish with parsley.

This would go well served with olive-oil sautéed potatoes, cooked together with the leaves from a finger-length sprig of rosemary.

Wine:
Given the rustic flavours here, the ideal option might be a sappy red Montepulciano d'Abbruzzo or a spicy Negroamaro wine from southern Italy.

Jarret d'agneau en Gasconnade

Serves 10

2 legs of spring lamb,
   shank end
2 tbsp olive oil
4 onions, sliced
3 carrots, sliced
1 leek (white part) sliced
1 turnip, sliced
3 tbsp plain flour
12 anchovy fillets,
   chopped
1 tbsp tomato paste

1 bottle of Cahors wine, or
   similar
peeled cloves of 1 bulb of
   garlic
3 tomatoes, peeled, seeded
   and chopped
bouquet garni
salt, pepper
light stock or water (if
   needed)

1   Preheat your oven to gas 3/325 F/170 C.
2   Sprinkle the lamb legs with salt and pepper. Heat the oil
    in a large heavy casserole and brown the lamb thoroughly
    on all sides to seal in the juices. Remove the meat from
    the pan and discard all but two tablespoonfuls of the fat.

3   Add the sliced onion, carrot, leek and turnip and cook them gently until soft. Stir in the flour, the chopped anchovies and the tomato purée or paste, and cook for 1 minute. Pour in the wine, bring everything up to the boil, and then allow to simmer gently for about 10 minutes.

4   At this stage stir in the peeled garlic cloves, the prepared tomatoes, the bouquet garni and some salt and pepper. Return the lamb shanks to the pan, adding a little stock or water if necessary to make sure they are completely covered.

5   Put the lid on the casserole and transfer it to the oven. Cook for 3 to 4 hours, turning the meat at intervals and adding stock or water if it shows signs of drying up.

6   At this stage the meat should be very tender. Remove the shanks to a warm covered dish whilst dealing with the sauce.

7   Remove the bouquet garni and correct the seasoning. If the sauce appears a bit thin, reduce it by fast boiling for a minute or two, and serve it over the meat.

8   Serve with an accompaniment of noodles.

Wine:
Either a spicy full-bodied wine from the Côteaux de Languedoc with plenty of presence (Pic-Saint-Loup, for example), or try a Côtes-du-Rhône Villages wine... Rasteau, perhaps.

Judy's savoury meat loaf

Slightly adapted, I have rescued this recipe from *The Pennywise Cookbook* published in 1973 by the Milk Marketing Board. The book itself is now dog-eared and food-stained from my wife Judy's recourse to it across the years, but the recipe has certainly stood the test of time as a simple, tasty and versatile family dish, to be enjoyed equally hot or sliced cold for a picnic with some cornichons, pickled onions and good crusty bread.

6 oz unsmoked streaky bacon, cut thin
8 oz minced steak (or equivalent cooked mince)
1 packet of bread sauce mix
Weetabix biscuit, crushed

1 tbsp chopped onion
1 tsp dried mixed herbs
1 tbsp concentrated tomato paste
5 fl oz milk
1 egg
salt, pepper

1   Butter a 5-inch cake or 1 lb loaf tin or use a smaller sized terrine mould.
2   Line the tin with streaky bacon rashers.

3   Mix together the minced meat, the dry bread sauce mix, the Weetabix, the chopped onion, the herbs and the tomato purée.

4   In a separate bowl beat the milk, egg and seasonings well together, and then add to the meat mixture. Blend together well.

5   Transfer this mixture to the prepared tin or terrine, cover with cooking foil and bake in a hot oven, gas 6/400 F/ 200 C, for about 1 hour.

Serve with sautéed potatoes and vegetables if hot, or with crisp salads if cold.

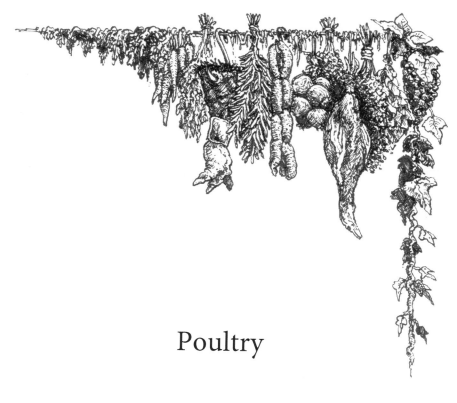

Poultry

Ferakh-al-hara (Moroccan chilli chicken)

The spicy heat of this dish can be varied according to the quantity of hot chilli powder used. The following recipe is only moderately hot.

Serves 4

5 tbsp olive oil
juice of a lemon
1 tsp chilli powder
salt, pepper

1 heaped tsp crushed
  garlic
1 free-range chicken,
  jointed
garnish of lemon wedges

1 Mix the olive oil, garlic, lemon juice, chilli powder and seasonings together in a bowl.
2 Put the chicken pieces in a fireproof baking dish and cover with this basting mixture.
3 Bake for 30 minutes in an oven at gas 5/375 F/190 C, basting the chicken for the first 15 minutes only... the idea is that the chicken should be reasonably crisp when cooked.

Serve accompanied by rice pilaf (see below), crisp green salad and Arabic bread.

Note:

If you have a steamer, put 5 oz of rice, a teaspoonful of cumin seeds (previously dry-fried for a few moments) and 10 fl oz of water in a bowl and place in the upper section of the steamer, adding sufficient water in the base of the steamer to permit steaming for around 25–30 minutes, by which time all the water in the top bowl should be absorbed into the rice, when it will have swollen to a fluffy fragrance; alternatively boil rice in the usual way, with the addition of a little spoonful of dry-fried cumin seeds.

Pollo 'al tegame'

A chicken fricassée with garlic and rosemary. One of my favourite dishes in its simplicity, and it tastes quintessentially 'Italian' in style.

Serves 4

1 good-sized free-range
  roasting chicken
1 oz butter
1 medium glass dry white
  wine

2 tbsp vegetable oil
3 cloves garlic, peeled
finger-length sprig of
  rosemary
salt, pepper

1   Cut the chicken into convenient pieces. Heat the butter and oil in a heavy casserole or a deep frying pan with a lid over medium heat. When the butter foam begins to subside add the garlic and the chicken pieces, skin side down. When the chicken is nicely browned on one side turn the pieces over and add the rosemary.

2   When the chicken pieces have taken colour all over, add a large pinch of salt, the pepper, and the wine. Let the wine bubble over the heat for two or three minutes and then substantially reduce the heat to a gentle simmer, and

cover the pan. The chicken should be tender in about 25 minutes.

3   Transfer the chicken pieces to a serving dish, discarding the garlic. Tilting the casserole, draw off any fat in excess of about 2 tablespoons. Bring the heat up again and add an equal quantity of water (or white wine) to deglaze the pan. Pour this as a sauce over the chicken.

Sautéed potatoes, green beans or broccoli seem to be good accompaniments.

Wine:
A simple unfussy Italian dry white: Nosiola from Trentino, or a classic local Trebbiano like Lugana DOC.

Algerian chicken sautée

Serves 6

1 large free-range chicken	500 g ripe tomatoes
6 fl oz olive oil	2 large aubergines
pinch saffron	4 capsicums: 2 red, 2 green
½ tsp cloves	3 cloves garlic
1 tsp cumin	2 tsp flour
1 lemon	flat-leaf parsley
4 large onions	salt, pepper

1 Cut the aubergines into smallish pieces and place them on a rack. Sprinkle salt over them and leave them to lose moisture for half an hour. Crush the cumin, cloves, garlic and saffron to a paste using a pestle and mortar.

2 Chop the onions, peel the tomatoes and chop the flesh. Cut the capsicums into strips, removing the seeds. In a large casserole sweat the chopped onion in about a third of the oil until translucent, and then add the chicken and the juice of the lemon. Lower the heat.

3 Pat the aubergine pieces dry with kitchen paper, and roll them in the flour. Heat another third of the oil in a separate saucepan and transfer the floured aubergine

pieces, cooking them on all sides, then add the capsicums, tomatoes, and the ground spices with the remaining third of the oil. Cover, and allow to cook very gently for 10 minutes.

4   Add the vegetable mixture to the chicken in its casserole and continue to cook gently for about 1 hour.

Arroz de galinha à Portuguesa (chicken rice, Portuguese style, from Alto Douro)

Although the Portuguese are famous for handling *bacalau* (salt cod) in 365 different ways, the country's diet remains bathed in simple rusticity for the main part, with an emphasis on the word 'simple'. Flavours are direct and usually uncomplicated.

I suggest the recipe below is one of the easiest all-in-one dishes to prepare and serve, though an additional green vegetable or mushrooms might not come amiss alongside.

Serves 4–6

1 medium chicken, cut up
    into serving pieces
3 oz (90 g) Spanish
    chorizo sausage (in lieu
    of the 'real thing', i.e.
    Portuguese *chouriço*)
3 oz (90 g) bacon lardons

14 oz rice
2 tbsp fruity olive oil
1 tbsp wine vinegar
1 large onion, chopped
1 tbsp flat-leaf parsley,
    chopped
salt, pepper

1 In a large pan, first fry the onion until golden, and then put in the lardons of bacon and the chicken pieces. Sauté for around 5 minutes, turning.

2 Add around ¼ pint (150 ml) of water, the vinegar and the chopped parsley, plus salt and pepper and cook very gently until half done.

3 Taste for seasoning and then add the rice and enough boiling water – or better still, use chicken stock – to cook it. (A rough guide is to use about 2½ times as much liquid by volume as the rice). Allow to cook gently until the rice is nearly tender, adding slices of chorizo sausage about 5 minutes before the dish is ready to serve.

4 The finished dish should be slightly wet, so have some further cooking liquid available if you think any needs to be added at the end.

Roast turkey, Lombardy style

The stuffing for this dish uses 'Luganega' sausages. Italian delis should be able to provide these spicy sausages in vacuum packs, or even freshly made – they get top marks for that!

NB: Start preparations 1 day in advance.

Serves 8

4–5 kg turkey, with giblets
6 slices Parma or San
 Daniele ham
1 finger-length sprig
 rosemary
12 sage leaves
150 g softened butter
1 medium onion
1 carrot
2 sticks celery
1 glass dry Marsala or
 sherry
½ bottle dry white wine
500 ml chicken stock (or
 dissolved cube)

1 heaped tsp cornflour or
 potato flour

for the stuffing:
500 g fresh Luganega
 sausages (see above)
100 g peeled cooked
 chestnuts
3 crisp eating apples,
 peeled and cored
8 stoned 'no-soak' prunes
1 measure brandy or
 grappa
1 lemon
50 g grated Parmesan
nutmeg, salt, pepper

1. First chop the prunes roughly and leave them to macerate in a bowl with the brandy for an hour or two in a cool place.

2. Skin the sausages and put the meat in a separate bowl with the lemon zest. Chop the turkey heart and liver into small dice and add these to the bowl, plus the coarsely chopped chestnuts.

3. Toss roughly chopped prepared apple in the lemon juice and add them to the mix, followed by the prunes in brandy, a good grating of nutmeg, plus the cheese. Mix well. (Fry a tiny bit of the stuffing to taste for seasoning – this will depend to some extent on the saltiness of the sausages.)

4. Push the stuffing into both cavities of the turkey, securing the flaps of skin with cocktail sticks (or even fine kitchen string on a bodkin or needle). Smear softened butter over the breast of the turkey until it is fully coated, season liberally with salt and pepper, and then distribute rosemary and sage leaves evenly across the surface. Finally, overlap the slices of Parma ham to cover the turkey breast completely.

5. The turkey is now ready for the oven, although the flavours would be more pronounced if it were left refrigerated overnight.

6. Preheat an oven to gas 6/400 F/200 C and roast the turkey undisturbed for half an hour, and then for a further two hours, basting it in its juices occasionally. Cover the breast lightly with foil if the ham threatens to burn. Then pour the fat out of the baking tray and reserve it.

7. Chop the carrot, onion and celery and lay them in the tray around the turkey. Cook everything together for a further ½ hour.

8 At this point the turkey should be done. Check by inserting a skewer between drumstick and thigh: the juices should run clear. If so, remove the turkey from the tray and keep it warm, covered loosely by foil.

9 Add the wine and the stock to the cooked vegetables, making sure the pan residues are scraped into them, and cook together over a medium heat until reduced and concentrated somewhat.

10 Mix the cornflour or potato flour with the Marsala or sherry and whisk it into the gravy. Simmer for a couple of minutes, adding any further juices that may have come from the turkey. Strain, and serve separately in a sauceboat.

Wine:
The full flavour of the turkey and stuffing seems to demand an equally fully flavoured red, preferably from Italy. Aglianico DOC from Basilicata, Taurasi from Campania, or a good Nero d'Avola from Sicily should do the trick.

Guinea fowl fricassée 'Burano style' (a prize-winner!)

Prompted by my wife Judy, I submitted this 'imagined' recipe to a competition, 'The Taste of Italy', run by the BBC in conjunction with Zanussi, the Italian kitchen suppliers. Judged by top chef Antonio Carluccio, it won me the first prize: a long gastronomic weekend for two in his company at the Cipriani Hotel, Venice. Clearly a bit of imagination pays off!

Serves 4

1 guinea fowl (Cornish hen) cut up into convenient pieces
1 tsp vinegar
2 carrots
1 stalk of celery
1 clove garlic
1 large onion
4 or 5 green olives
6 capers
6 sage leaves

1 tbsp fresh rosemary
1 Italian (or Toulouse) fresh pork sausage
2 slices pancetta, or green bacon
2 tbsp olive oil
5 fl oz dry white wine
juice of half a lemon
a small strip of lemon zest
1 small tot of grappa (or brandy)

1 Put the guinea fowl pieces in a bowl of water acidulated with the vinegar and allow to steep for about half an hour.

2 Finely chop the carrots, celery, garlic, onion, olives, capers, herbs, sausage and pancetta, and mix them all together in a separate bowl.

3 Heat the oil in a fricassée pan. Pat the guinea fowl sections dry with a paper towel and put them in the pan together with all the chopped ingredients. Let them take colour briefly, then reduce the heat under the pan. Turn the ingredients from time to time and let them cook gently together until pale gold in colour.

4 Add the white wine, the lemon juice, the strip of lemon zest and the grappa, making sure the fluids are well mixed in. Cover the pan and allow to simmer on a very gentle heat until the guinea fowl is tender.

Wine:
I'd suggest a Gavi di Gavi from Piedmont, or a top quality Pinot Grigio from Friuli (Collio).

Alsace-style braised guinea fowl

Serves 4

1 guinea fowl (Cornish
   hen)
1 medium red onion
   studded with 4 cloves
50 g bacon, diced
1 small cabbage
4 small or 2 large carrots,
   sliced
1 tbsp vegetable oil
600 ml chicken broth

300 ml Alsace lager beer
2 fresh pork sausages
   (Toulouse variety)
a bouquet garni of parsley,
   thyme and bay leaf
½ tsp *quatre épices* (see
   page 123)
salt, pepper

1   Truss the hen and blanch the bacon slices. Cut up the
    cabbage and slice the carrots. Place the clove-stuck onion
    in the cavity of the bird.

2   Heat the oil in a heavy-bottomed casserole and brown the
    guinea fowl on all sides; remove it from the pan and add
    the bacon pieces to the oil, letting them take on a little
    colour.

3   Add half the sliced cabbage and half the sliced carrots to the pan, season with salt and pepper, and replace the fowl on the top. Surround the bird with the remaining vegetables, season with more salt and pepper and the *quatre épices* (alternatively use the same quantity of Chinese five-spice powder or powdered cloves). Add the chicken broth and the lager beer to the pan and then add a bouquet garni to the vegetables in the pan, making sure it is well tucked in. Cover the casserole and allow to simmer very gently for about 1¼ hours.

4   Meanwhile, blanch the sausages to stiffen them, cut them in chunks and reserve them, adding them to the casserole during the last 15 minutes of cooking.

5   When the guinea fowl is tender, remove it from the casserole and keep it warm. Remove and discard the bouquet garni. Strain the cooking juices from the vegetables into a small pan and boil up vigorously until reduced by half. Meanwhile, make sure the vegetables are kept warm. Adjust the sauce seasoning if necessary and strain it.

6   Transfer the vegetables to a warmed serving dish and place the guinea fowl on top, either as it is or cut up into convenient serving pieces. Add a little of the sauce to moisten and pass the rest around in a sauceboat.

Serve accompanied by new potatoes with parsley garnish.

Wine:
Either Alsace Pinot Blanc... or a light Alsace beer.

Quatre épices Alsacien

A distinctive 'four spice' flavouring used particularly in French *charcuterie*. *Quatre épices* has a multitude of uses in spicing classic French savoury dishes, and keeps well in a tightly stoppered jar.

The quantities of *quatre épices* are:

2 tsp ground black pepper
1 tsp ground nutmeg

½ tsp ground cloves
¼ tsp ground ginger

… or in proportion.

Gressingham duck in Sauvignon de Loire

NB: Requires initial preparation 24 hours in advance.

Serves 2

One Gressingham or
  Barbary duck
100 ml of eau de vie de
  mirabelle (or Cognac)
2 carrots
1 onion
1 turnip
1 clove garlic
parsley
2 tbsp vegetable oil

a bay leaf
a sprig of thyme
6 coriander seeds
600 ml stock
600 ml Sauvignon blanc
  (or other crisp white
  wine)
dash white wine vinegar
1 tsp sugar

1   Pour the *eau de vie* or Cognac inside the duck… slosh it
    around a bit… and allow the duck to marinate for 24
    hours, turning it from time to time to allow all the inner
    surfaces to absorb the alcohol/aromatics.

2   The following day, prepare the vegetables: grate the carrot and turnip, and finely chop the onion and the garlic.

3   In an ovenproof casserole, heat the oil and brown the duck on all sides, removing the residual fat in the pan once the duck is browned.

4   Add a little vinegar and sugar to the duck in the pan to make a light caramel.

5   Add the chopped and grated vegetables plus the herbs and spice, then pour in the stock and wine, cover and allow to cook gently, covered, for about 1½ hours.

6   Remove the duck and keep it warm. Meanwhile reduce the sauce to approx ½ pint by fast boiling.

7   Carve the duck or cut into convenient pieces and mask with the sauce. Serve with steamed new potatoes and glazed turnips.

Wine:

A good Loire Sauvignon, perhaps a Sancerre, Pouilly-Fumé or a Quincy.

American roast duck

This is a successful amalgam of two separate American recipes for duckling... this one has a nut stuffing and an apricot glaze and sauce.

duckling weighing about
  2 kg
giblets
salt

for stuffing:
the duck liver
25 g butter
a medium-sized onion,
  peeled and chopped
1 stick celery, sliced
100 g fresh breadcrumbs
25 g chopped pecans or
  walnuts

1 egg, lightly beaten
1 tbsp fresh chopped
  parsley
salt, pepper

for apricot glaze and sauce:
5 tbsp apricot jam
300 ml duck giblet stock
juice and grated rind of
  ½ lemon
25 g cornflour or
  arrowroot
salt, pepper

1   Wipe the duck dry with a kitchen towel then rub salt into its skin.

2   Put the giblets in a pan, cover with water and bring gently up to a boil. Cover the pan and leave to simmer very gently for 45 minutes. Strain into a bowl. Chop the duck liver and reserve it in another bowl.

3   Heat butter in a small pan and sauté the chopped onion and celery until softened but not browned...about 5 minutes, say. Add this to the chopped duck liver along with the breadcrumbs, nuts, egg, parsley and seasonings and mix together to make a fairly dry stuffing. Pack this into the cavity of the duck and truss it up tidily.

4   Put the stuffed duck on a wire rack in a roasting pan and begin roasting it at 400F / 200C (gas mark 6) for about 10 minutes. Reduce the heat to 350F / 180C (gas mark 4) and cook for a further hour, basting it from time to time with its pan juices.

5   Meanwhile make the apricot glaze: Reduce together to apricot jam with the duck stock and use a little of this mixture to baste the duck during its last 15 minutes cooking, keeping the remainder aside for the sauce: put the glaze in a small pan. Put the cornflour or arrowroot in a cup with a few tablespoons of the duck stock, stirring it until it is smooth, and then add it to the pan with the remainder of the stock and apricot glaze. Cook until the mixture thickens, stirring constantly.

Wine:
Nothing too severe or tannic, plenty of ripe fruit. Californian Zinfandel is ideal, but a freshly fruity Beaujolais, or a Dolcetto from Piedmont would do very nicely too.

Roast partridge with muscat grapes

This simple but tasty recipe is remembered from a meal taken at the Hotel dos Reyes Catolicos in Santiago di Compostela in Galicia – one of Spain's fine chain of parador hotels.

Serves 4

4 partridges, plucked,
    drawn and dressed
salt, pepper
40 g butter
50 ml dry sherry

50 ml game stock – or
    substitute chicken stock
200 g white muscatel
    grapes

1   Season the partridges inside and out with salt and pepper, truss them, and sauté them on both sides in butter in a casserole until their skins are gently browned all over.

2   Take the partridges out of the casserole, remove their trussing strings and keep them warm while you add the sherry to the cooking juices in the pan.

3   Add the game (or chicken) stock and the muscatel grapes.

4   Return the partridges to the casserole and check that the stock is sufficiently seasoned.

5   Cover the casserole with a lid and bake in a hot oven (gas 7/425 F/220 C) for ten minutes.

Serve direct from the casserole, accompanying each partridge with a golden chunk of caramelised butternut squash (see next recipe), and with a discreet pool of *salsa verde* (see page 37) alongside.

Note:

The cooking time for the partridges may seem alarmingly short, but they should be served fairly rare.

Caramelised
butternut squash

The perfect accompaniment to the roast partridge recipe on page 128.

Serves 4

2 kg butternut squash, peeled	25 g unsalted butter
	1 tbsp clear honey

1. Cut the squash in half along its length and remove its seeds. Cut it into four evenly sized pieces.
2. In a small pan melt the butter with the honey and brush the mixture over the segments of squash. Season to taste. Transfer the pieces to a baking tray and roast in a hot oven (gas 7/425 F/220 C) for about 12–15 minutes.

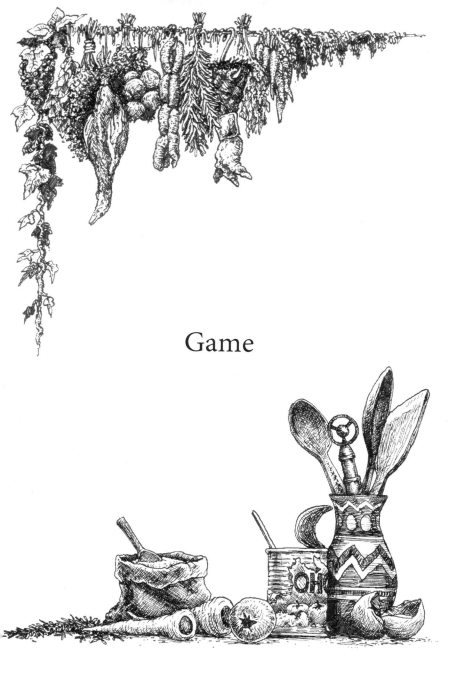

Game

Lapin sauté à la Bordelaise

Simple countrified stuff, this. The recipe comes from the wife of the owner of a wine property in Fronsac, on the right bank of the Gironde, Bordeaux.

Serves 2–3

a rabbit of about 1½ kg
olive oil
seasoned flour
1 complete head of garlic
fresh thyme

bay leaf
salt, pepper
1 glass of dry white wine
parsley, chopped, for
   decoration

1   Cut up the rabbit into six pieces. Roll in seasoned flour. Sauté in oil in a large fireproof pan or casserole over high heat until well browned on all sides, then lower the heat. At this point add crushed garlic, a few good sprigs of fresh thyme, a bay leaf and salt and pepper. Pour a glass of dry white wine over the casserole, cover, and allow to cook very gently for 30–40 minutes.
2   Decorate with fresh chopped parsley.

3   Serve with steamed new potatoes, carrots and fresh peas
     – or why not try baby leeks cooked in red wine? Cut up
     your leeks into 1-inch lengths, sauté briefly in hot oil
     until browned on all sides, then moisten with equal
     proportions of red wine and vegetable or chicken stock.
     Cook down until nicely glazed.

Wine:

Ideally a 'right-bank' Bordeaux from Fronsac, or the Côtes de
Blaye.

Rabbit as tuna
(coniglio tonnato)

The Italians have a love of tuna: and not simply for itself, fresh from the sea, but as the main ingredient in a sauce for rumps of veal as in *vitello tonnato,* backed up with the additional flavouring of capers. (Italy's Aeolian Islands are renowned for the very best caper buds!)

Here I include a cost-effective dish straight from an inland Italian *trattoria* which adapts itself wonderfully, if garlickly, to a cold summer table.

NB: Maceration time, three days.

Serves 8–10 as a starter or part of a buffet table

1 rabbit	1 litre of extra virgin
25 sage leaves	olive oil
1 head of garlic	salt, pepper

1   Divide the rabbit into pieces and put these in a pan. Cover with salted water and bring to a very gentle simmer for about 40 minutes. By this time the meat should be soft and on the point of falling off the bone.

Drain the rabbit pieces, and while still warm pull the flesh off the bones.

2 Put a layer of rabbit meat in an earthenware pot, top it with a layer of fresh uncrushed garlic cloves and sage leaves, plus some seasoning of salt and pepper, and then repeat the process until you have used up all the meat. Depending on the size of the dish you should aim to get three layers. Cover with a good fruity olive oil and leave to infuse for about *three days* in a refrigerator.

3 A good crusty bread seems obligatory alongside, and I think it is a good plan to serve this with the contrast of a salad comprising some bitter leaves, chicory or radicchio perhaps, to give a vibrant taste and texture perspective to the garlic-infused oil.

Wine:

The robust flavours of the marinated rabbit would match a robust southern Italian white wine like Sicilian Grillo, or a Falanghina from Campania.

Lapin à deux moutardes

There is little doubt that mustard enlivens the flavour of rabbit and is an ingredient frequently used in classic French recipes involving this delicately flavoured animal. The recipe that follows is a 'remembered' version of one published by Robert Carrier in his *Great Dishes of the World* in the early sixties. I can only say that it worked well when I cooked it originally; and, although my copy of the book has long since fallen apart through usage, the recipe still seems to have a classic integrity that confirms it as a delicious dish for the table today. Here goes!

1 rabbit (preferably wild, not farmed)
2 tbsp flour
seasonings of salt and pepper
2 tbsp olive oil
2 tbsp butter
4 oz bacon, diced and blanched
4 shallots, finely diced

a bouquet garni
a glass of white wine (¼ pint or thereabouts)
same amount of chicken stock
a heaped tsp of Dijon mustard
a heaped tsp of English mustard
10 oz double cream

1 Divide the rabbit into serving portions, roll them in seasoned flour, and sauté them in the oil and butter with the diced bacon until coloured. Add the shallots and the bouquet garni and then add the wine and the stock to the pan. Cook *very gently*, covered, until the rabbit is tender.

2 Remove the rabbit pieces and keep them warm. At this point remove the bouquet garni and skim any excess fat from the sauce. Add both mustards to the cream, stir to incorporate well and then add this mixture to the sauce in the pan. Check for seasoning and then introduce the cooked rabbit pieces to the pan. Heat through, and serve.

I'd suggest that *pommes fondants* and steamed Kenya beans might go particularly well with this dish.

Wine:
A sappy fresh Loire red like Chinon or Bourgeuil.

Wild rabbit and porcini ragù

This recipe looks more complicated than it is! Delicious though the classic Tuscan *pappardelle alla lepre* may be, I fight shy of cooking hares on the grounds that they are not only beautiful animals but they are relatively rare. Wild rabbits are plentiful and are quite a different matter, and I was delighted to find an alternative recipe using wild rabbit, enhanced by the earthy taste of porcini mushrooms. There is certainly no loss of 'wild' (and authentically Tuscan) flavouring here.

1 wild rabbit, cut into
  portions
3 tbsp olive oil
150 g unsmoked bacon
  lardons (or use pancetta)
250 g chestnut
  mushrooms, sliced
100 g dried ceps (porcini)
2 'banana' shallots – or a
  medium onion

2 fat garlic cloves, crushed
60 ml white wine vinegar
120 ml dry white wine
500 ml chicken or
  vegetable stock
bouquet garni comprising
  1 bay leaf, 3 sprigs of
  thyme, 2 sprigs of sage
  and 1 sprig of rosemary

1   Cut the rabbit into pieces. Season well with salt and pepper. Soak the dried porcini mushrooms in 240 ml of hot water. Cut the fresh mushrooms into slices about as thick as a pound coin. Chop the shallots or onion into cubes. Peel and crush the 2 garlic cloves.

2   Add the olive oil to a large ovenproof casserole pan, heating it on top of the oven to the point it gives off a haze. Add the rabbit pieces and brown them thoroughly on all sides for around 10–12 minutes.

3   Once the rabbit has taken colour all over, remove it from the pan and keep it warm in a dish. Add the bacon lardons to the same pan and let them brown well in the oil. Add the shallots or onion and let them cook with the bacon until showing caramelised golden-brown edges.

4   Add both the vinegar and the wine to the pan and stir well to scrape up any residues sticking to the bottom of the pan. Reduce heat a little and simmer until the liquid is reduced to a mere tablespoonful. At this point add the stock and the bouquet garni of fresh herbs. Simmer for a minute or two, then check seasoning.

5   Add the chopped fresh mushrooms together with the soaked porcini mushrooms along with their soaking liquid. Reintroduce the browned rabbit to the pan. Combine all the elements in the pan, and cover it with a sheet of foil, then the lid, to ensure a good airtight seal. Put the pan to braise in an oven at gas 3/325 F/170 C for about an hour.

6   Once the hour is up, remove the pan from the oven, extract the rabbit pieces and set them aside to cool a little. Then, using two forks, tease and scrape the rabbit meat from the bones, returning the shredded meat to the pan. Discard the rabbit bones.

7   You could finish here, but I usually allow the mixed ingredients to simmer together very gently, under cover,

for a further 15–20 minutes to ensure that the rabbit meat is softened sufficiently and adequately takes up the flavourings of the sauce.

Serve with pappardelle pasta ribbons. Hand round grated Parmesan cheese separately, and season with a little freshly ground black pepper.

Faisan à la Normande

This is a classic French regional dish. The description 'à la Normande' frequently refers to the use either of apples, cider or Calvados in a recipe, and cream usually comes somewhere into the picture too.

Serves 6

2 pheasants
75 g butter
100 ml Calvados (or brandy)
4 tart eating apples, Granny Smith perhaps

250 g dry cider
200 g crème fraîche
juice of half a lemon
salt, pepper

1 Melt the butter in a flameproof casserole large enough to hold both birds, and brown them all over.

2 Pour in the Calvados or brandy and set light to it. (Watch those eyebrows!)

3 When the flames have died down, turn the birds breast side down in the pan and tuck slices from two of the apples, previously peeled and cored, around them. Season with salt and pepper.

4   Pour the cider over the pheasants, cover the dish and cook at gas 4/350 F/180 C for about 30 minutes, turning the birds the other way up halfway through the cooking process.

5   While the pheasants are cooking, fry slices of the remaining two apples in butter until browned and set them aside.

6   When the pheasants are cooked, take them out of their casserole and transfer them to a serving dish. Surround them with the fried apple slices and keep them warm.

7   Put the casserole on a medium heat on the hob, adding cream or *crème fraîche* to the apples already in the pan. Bring to a boil and stir everything well together until reduced to a good consistency for a sauce. Press through a sieve if necessary to ensure smoothness.

8   Adjust seasoning, adding a dash of lemon juice to 'lift' the flavours.

9   Serve the pheasants surrounded with a little sauce, and hand around the remainder separately.

Wild duck with port and orange sauce

Serves 2

2 wild duck, oven dressed
4 shallots, finely chopped
350 ml fresh orange juice
350 ml port
zest and juice of 1 orange

2 tbsp *crème fraîche* or
   thick cream
salt, pepper

1   Roast the birds in the centre of a hot oven (gas 7/425 F/ 220 C) for 45 minutes, pouring the orange juice over them after about 20 minutes' cooking time. Baste the ducks during the remaining cooking period, then remove from the oven and keep warm.

2   In a separate saucepan have the pared zest and juice of the orange, the port wine, and the chopped shallots. Pour into this the orange/cooking juices from the duck, skimming as much fat off as possible.

3   Reduce by boiling hard, then remove from the heat and add the cream and seasonings, stirring over low heat until the sauce is properly amalgamated.

4   Serve with a watercress and orange-slice garnish, a purée of celeriac, and a julienne of carrots and Kenya beans.

Wine:
Carmenère, Los Robles, Chile; or 'Celèbre' Cabernet/Shiraz, Martinborough, New Zealand.

Schwartzwalder Rehpfeffer (Black Forest peppered venison casserole)

Prepare a day ahead.

Serves 4–6

1 kg venison, cubed
16 fl oz dry red wine
3 bay leaves
8 juniper berries, crushed
½ tsp dried thyme
1 onion studded with
  6 cloves
6 black peppercorns
2 slivers of lemon peel

125 g speck (or smoked
  bacon), diced
salt, pepper
500 ml beef stock
100 ml soured cream
3 tbsp redcurrant jelly
freshly ground white
  pepper, to taste
½ tsp grated lemon zest

1   The day beforehand, place the cubed meat in a marinade of wine, crushed juniper berries, bay leaves, thyme, onion and cloves, peppercorns and lemon peel. Refrigerate for up to 24 hours.

2   Drain the meat and reserve the marinade.

3   Lightly sauté the speck or bacon to render the fat. Set the bacon aside.

4   In the same pan add the venison in batches, and fry until seized on all sides.

5   Return the bacon, stir and add 1 cup of beef stock.

6   Cover the pan and simmer over a low heat for about 1 hour or until the meat is tender. During this time gradually add the reserved marinade, strained.

7   Add the sour cream, the redcurrant jelly and the grated lemon zest, plus sufficient freshly ground white pepper to make the stew sufficiently peppery (to taste).

8   Mix well, and allow to cook gently for a further 5 minutes.

Suggestion:
Serve with noodles and a stew of apples and cranberries, only slightly sweetened.

Wine:
A rich-textured off-dry white wine: Rheingau QmP Riesling Auslese, or a late harvest Tokay/Pinot Gris from Alsace.

Tuscan wild boar casserole

Prepare a day ahead. A true taste of winter in Tuscany!

Serves 2–3

500 g cubed wild boar
1 tbsp olive oil
½ tbsp flour
200 ml hearty red wine
salt
black pepper

for the marinade:
1 onion, chopped
1 good clove of garlic,
    skinned and crushed
6 juniper berries, crushed
1 bay leaf
leaves from a good sprig of
    rosemary
1 tbsp olive oil
1 tbsp hearty red wine
1 tbsp red wine vinegar

1   Put the meat into a ceramic or glass bowl and add the ingredients for the marinade. Cover, and leave in a cool place for 24 hours.

2   Drain the meat from the marinade and pat it dry with paper towels. Reserve the marinade.

3   Once dry, dredge the meat lightly with the flour. Heat oil in a heavy-based frying pan and fry the meat in batches until each batch browns all over, removing the meat to an earthenware *marmite* or casserole dish. Deglaze the frying pan with the marinade and wine, and pour over the meat in the casserole.

4   Make sure the casserole is well sealed for slow cooking by placing a double layer of kitchen foil under the lid, and cook in a very slow oven (gas 1/250 F/130 C) for around 2 hours until the meat is very tender and the sauce is well reduced to be little more than a covering for the meat.

5   Season to taste and serve on a bed of noodles or with polenta.

My suggested garnish is of butter-glazed peeled apple slices, lightly spiced with cinnamon.

Wine:
Something classically Sangiovese-based: Morellino di Scansano DOC or a Vino Nobile di Montepulciano DOCG.

Breads, cakes,
biscuits and sundries

Parmesan and pine-nut biscottini with green olives

These little savoury nibbles are great favourites as part of a slew of dry canapés, and I usually partner them with sesame and Roquefort biscuits (see page 152).

Makes about 40–50

100 g pine nuts, lightly
  toasted in the oven
250 g plain flour
1 tsp baking powder
1 tsp salt
¼ tsp fresh ground black
  pepper

1 tbsp fennel seeds
2 tbsp freshly grated
  Parmesan cheese
100 g pitted green olives,
  chopped finely
2 eggs, beaten

1   Preheat the oven to gas 4/350 F/180 C.

2   Spread the pine nuts across a baking tray and toast in the oven for around 5 minutes until golden. Allow to cool.

3   Sift flour, baking powder and salt into a bowl. Add the fennel seeds, pepper, Parmesan and the olives. Mix together with the 3 beaten eggs to form a rough dough.

Alternatively use a food processor to whizz the above ingredients together.

4   Knead the toasted pine nuts into the dough and divide it into four. Roll each segment out on a floured board into a log approx 12 inches long, and transfer each one to a prepared baking sheet covered either with baking parchment or some other proprietary non-stick covering. (Alternatively use a baking sheet dusted with flour to prevent sticking.)

5   Bake for approx 25 minutes until firm to the touch. Remove from the oven and allow to cool.

6   Once cool enough to handle, cut each log on the diagonal into ¼-inch slices using a sharp serrated bread knife. Place the slices in a single layer on the baking sheet and return to the oven for around 10–15 minutes until the *biscotti* are crisp and dry.

7   Cool completely on a wire rack, and serve sprinkled with a little sea salt.

Sesame and Roquefort biscuits

This very simple biscuit recipe comes originally from Shaun Hill, formerly *chef de cuisine* at Gidleigh Park, Devon and subsequently of The Merchant House, Ludlow, and appears to be one of his staple *amuse-bouches* over the years. One of the benefits for busy party cooks is that the raw biscuit mixture can be prepared several days in advance and stored in the fridge until needed.

Makes about 20 biscuits

100 g unsalted butter
100 g self-raising flour

100 g Roquefort (or other strongly flavoured blue cheese)
50 g sesame seeds

1   Whizz the flour and butter together in a food processor until the mixture resembles fine breadcrumbs. Crumble the cheese into the mixture and whizz again very briefly (2 to 3 seconds only, simply to ensure even distribution

of the ingredients). Refrigerate if you wish to store the mixture for later use.

2 Pinch out small pieces of the dough and roll them into small balls anything from 1½ to 2 cm across, and toss them in sesame seeds.

3 Spread these pastry balls evenly on a greased baking sheet (or use baking parchment) and cook in a gas 4/350 F/ 180 C oven for about 10 minutes, or until the biscuits appear firm.

Tasted fresh, they are *wonderful* – very moreish as part of a selection of canapés.

Shaun Hill's walnut & rosemary bread

Unless using ½ oz of fresh yeast, which the author recommends, I use a teaspoonful of 'quick-rise' dry yeast added to the dry ingredients.

454 g granary flour	250 ml warmed milk
50 g chopped walnuts	sprig of fresh rosemary
50 g unsalted butter	yeast (see above)
50 g soft brown sugar	salt

1. Melt the butter in a small pan with the rosemary until the butter browns to a light *noisette*, then add the sugar and the milk.
2. Allow to cool until tepid, then strain through a sieve onto the flour which has had the yeast and salt added to it.
3. Knead in the chopped walnuts.
4. Cover, and allow to double in volume.
5. Knock back. Shape into loaves and allow a further rise, then bake for 15–20 minutes in a gas 6/400 F/200 C oven.

Norfolk spelt bread

Why Norfolk? Simply because the mill at Letheringsett produces *the* ideal spelt flour for bread-making purposes.

NB: This bread tastes exceptionally good toasted!

350 g spelt flour, sifted
a good teaspoon of salt
1 tsp English mustard
  powder
40 g soft salted butter
50 g walnuts, chopped
25 g sultanas (optional)

10 g fresh yeast, or
  1 sachet dried
1 tsp caster sugar
120–150 ml lukewarm
  milk & water in equal
  proportions
1 beaten egg

1   Mix together the dry ingredients plus the butter (and dried yeast, if using) in the bowl of a food mixer. Using a dough hook, blend thoroughly together. Pour about 120 ml of the warmed milk/water mix into a separate bowl with the beaten egg.

2   If using fresh yeast, combine it with the sugar in a bowl and mix with your fingertips until it becomes smooth and almost liquid; then add about 120 ml of the warm milk/water mix, plus the beaten egg.

3   Next, with the mixer running, pour the warm liquid onto the flour to make a soft dough, and allow the machine to knead the dough until it comes away from the sides of the bowl. (This may take anything between 5 and 8 minutes, by which time the dough should become a springy homogenous mass – not sticking to your fingers!)

4   Remove the bowl from the mixer and cover it with a damp tea-towel. Leave in a warm place for about an hour, or until the dough has doubled in volume.

5   Remove the dough from the bowl and shape it into a rough rectangle on a baking tray. The dough will have shrunk when you disturb it, so leave it on the tray uncovered in a warm place for around 45 minutes to prove and double its size again.

6   Place the tray in a pre-heated hot oven (gas 7/425 F/ 220 C) and bake for 20–25 minutes.

7   Cool the loaf on a wire rack.

Brandysnaps with thyme and cumin

I make this variant on the classic brandysnap recipe to accompany a compôte of dried fruits macerated with a few spices in port or Madeira (a Delia Smith Christmas 'standby') which I think goes particularly well with clove-flavoured ice cream (see page 194).

At first sight the addition of pungent aromatic or herbal flavours to a toffee-sweet buttery biscuit may seem a little strange. 'Futurist' Italian cook Marinetti might well have gone much further back in the 1920s out of a desire to shock fellow Italians out of eating pasta, as might today's chefs at the cutting edge of flavour/texture perceptions like René Redzepi at Copenhagen's Noma, and Heston Blumenthal at The Fat Duck at Bray where combinations of sweet and savoury appear with astonishing effect.

This herbal brandysnap recipe of my own is not quite in the same league of outrageousness... sorry, bravery!

60 g unsalted butter
60 g caster sugar
60 g plain flour
2 tbsp golden syrup
½ tsp powdered ginger

1 tsp brandy
1 tsp dried thyme
½ tsp cumin seeds
pinch of salt

1   Melt the butter with the caster sugar over a low heat, making sure that the mixture is smooth. Sieve the flour and ginger into the mix. Stir until well incorporated and then add the golden syrup, the brandy, the thyme and the cumin seeds. Ensure everything is well blended. Cook gently together for a minute or two. Season very lightly with salt.

2   Prepare a baking tray either with a proprietary non-stick Teflon sheet or baking parchment, and drop heaped teaspoonfuls of the mixture onto it, well spaced to allow for 'spread' when cooking.

3   Put into a heated oven at gas 5/375 F/190 C for about 5 minutes until the mixture creeps out into lacy golden circles. Don't forget that sugar tends to 'catch', so keep an eye on them.

4   Meanwhile grease a few wooden spoon handles, or the base of small moulds if you are going to form cups. Once cooked and hot out of the oven the brandysnaps can then be folded round them with a palette knife and allowed to set into the shape you want.

Biscotti di prato (cantuccine)

Makes 20+ biscuits

100 g blanched almonds
450 g unbleached plain
  flour
150 g granulated sugar
3 eggs (size 2)
pinch salt
1 tsp baking powder

1 egg white, beaten

optional:
50 g dark chocolate chips,
  or chopped glacé fruits

1   Preheat oven to fairly hot (gas 5/375 F/190 C).
2   Toast the almonds in the oven until the nuts are golden:
    about 10–15 minutes… but keep an eye on them so that
    they don't burn.
3   Grind about a third of the toasted almonds very fine, and
    coarsely chop the remainder.
4   On a pastry board make a mound of the flour, put a well
    in it and add to it all the ground and chopped almonds,
    the sugar, eggs, salt and baking powder. Make sure the
    mixture in the well is sufficiently stirred, then start
    incorporating the flour little by little until you have a
    homogenous dough. (NB: If you're planning to add

chocolate 'bits' or glacé fruits to your *biscotti* they should go in when all but 2 tbsp of the flour has been fully incorporated to the basic dough mix.) Knead the dough for a couple of minutes and then divide it into 4 pieces, shaping each one by hand into a thin roll about ½ inch in diameter.

5   Prepare a baking sheet by lightly buttering and flouring it, and place the rolls on it. In a separate bowl, beat the egg white until frothy, and brush the tops of the four rolls with it. Bake in the oven (gas 5/375 F/190 C) for 20 minutes.

6   Remove the rolls from the oven and, with a long knife, cut a 45 degree diagonal angle in the *biscotti* every ¼ inch along the roll. Return them to a cooler oven (225 F/ 100 C) and bake for a further 30 minutes.

Allow to cool down completely before serving. *Biscotti* keep quite well stored in an airtight stoppered jar.

Best served 'dunked' in a glass of Vin Santo, Passito di Pantelleria, or other dessert wine.

Panforte di Siena

I admit a weakness for this delicious Tuscan 'nougat' which comes into its own at Christmas time. My dentist has strongly warned me against it, but I usually weaken. The recipe I use nowadays is that of Ursula Ferrigno, in her book *Italy from Sea to Sky* – and is arguably the most authentic replication of genuine *panforte*. So be it. *Buon Natale!*

4 oz (115 g) hazelnuts, toasted
4 oz (115 g) blanched toasted almonds
1½ oz (35 g) each of candied apricots, ginger and dried figs, chopped
4 oz (125 g) mixed citrus peel
1 tsp ground cinnamon
½ tsp each of ground coriander, ground cloves and fresh grated nutmeg

3 pinches of freshly ground black pepper
3¼ oz (90 g) breadmaking flour or 'Tipo 00'
5 oz (150 g) unrefined granulated sugar
4½ oz (125 g) aromatic honey (I use dark Greek honey)
1½ oz (35 g) unsalted butter
icing sugar to dust

1   Have your oven at gas 4/350 F/180 C.

2   Line an 8-inch diameter springform cake tin with baking parchment.

3   Mix the prepared toasted nuts and all the candied fruit with the flour in a bowl; amalgamate well.

4   Meanwhile put the sugar, honey and butter into a heavy-bottomed saucepan and cook until the mixture attains a temperature of 116 C (soft ball).

5   Once this target is reached – and don't go any further unless you want to incur the displeasure of your dentist – pour this syrup onto the nut/fruit mixture and combine well.

6   Transfer to the prepared baking tin. Fast work is required here, as the cooling mixture will quickly become stiffer.

7   Put the tin in the preheated low oven and cook for approx 30–40 minutes.

8   Allow to cool in the tin until firm, and then either cut the *panforte* up into individual pieces or remove it to a dish and, once cooled down completely, dust it with icing sugar.

Spiced nuts

A 'recipe' adopted by chef-restaurateur Sally Clarke from a former member of her staff, and dreadfully moreish as nibbles, especially around Christmas!

200 g of mixed shelled
 nuts – your own choice
1 tbsp of rosemary, finely
 chopped
¼ tsp cayenne pepper

1½ tsp muscovado sugar
1 tsp salt (I use Maldon
 salt for preference)
½ tsp creamed garlic
½ tsp walnut or olive oil

1 Mix all the ingredients together. Spread on a baking tray and bake in the oven (gas 3/325 F/170 C) for 10 minutes.

2 Remove from the oven, stir the nuts around to expose another surface and return to the oven for a further 10 minutes.

3 Allow the nuts to cool completely on the tray.

Note:
Best eaten the same day as prepared; the salty/spicy/smoky/nutty flavours suggest a good dry *almacenista* oloroso sherry alongside, or perhaps a nutty dry Sercial Madeira.

Desserts and ice creams

Patty Green's spiced pan-roasted apple cake

A recipe generously donated by a good friend and excellent cook.

Serves 6

4 apples (Granny Smith), peeled, cored and sliced into 6
250 g soft brown sugar
100 g unsalted butter
150 g plain flour
350 g caster sugar
2 tsp ground cinnamon
2 tsp mixed spice

1 heaped tsp baking powder
½ tsp salt
2 large eggs
5 fl oz corn oil
1 apple (Granny Smith), coarse grated
1 heaped tsp grated ginger

1   Preheat oven to gas 4/350 F/180 C. Sprinkle the soft brown sugar over the bottom of a heavy 12-inch pan – one with a good depth if possible. Add butter to the pan and place in the oven for about 5 minutes to allow the butter and sugar to melt together.

2   In a separate bowl mix together the flour, the caster sugar, the spices, baking powder and salt. Beat in the eggs and the oil, then fold in the grated apple and the ginger.

3   Remove the melted butter/sugar from the oven and whisk the mixture until the sugar is well dissolved and no longer granular.

4   Arrange the sliced apples neatly on the bottom of the pan.

5   Pour the batter over the apples and bake until the cake is springy to the touch – about 1 hour. Test with a skewer: it will come out clean if the cake is done.

6   Cool slightly, turn out onto a plate or cakestand, and serve warm with *crème fraîche* alongside.

Note:

You may omit the ginger if you wish.

The dish also works very successfully with pears.

Strudel aux Quetsches

Serves 4–6

800 g Quetsch or Victoria
  plums
200 ml red wine
100 g caster sugar
75 g unsalted butter
2 pinches of cinnamon
1 pinch mixed spice

6 sheets filo pastry
melted butter to brush
  over
1 egg yolk, thinned with a
  few drops of water
2 tbsp flaked almonds

1 Stone and quarter the plums and cook them briefly in the wine and sugar.

2 Remove them from the pan with a slotted spoon and in a separate pan fry them briefly in half the butter and the spices.

3 Leave them to cool. Meanwhile reduce the wine/sugar syrup until thickened and whisk in the rest of the butter.

4 Lay out the filo sheets, overlapping them very slightly, and paint them with melted butter; six thicknesses should be about right.

5 Arrange the cooled cooked plums over the pastry, leaving a clear border of about 1½ to 2 inches. Turn the long

sides inwards and roll up the pastry from a short end as if for a Swiss roll. Put the strudel, seam side down, on an oiled baking sheet, brush it with the beaten egg yolk, press the almonds on top and put in the fridge to chill until needed for cooking.

6   Cook in a hot oven (gas 7/425 F/220 C) for about 20 minutes. Warm up the reduced wine syrup and serve alongside. This works well with an accompaniment of fresh vanilla ice cream.

Little pots of chocolate Cognac creams

Hah! Simple luxury!! A recipe from *The Women Chefs of Britain* published by Absolute Press.
(May even be made a couple of days in advance.)

Serves 6

350 g top quality
  plain chocolate
  (70–72% solids)
1 pint single cream

2 eggs
salt
4 tbsp brandy

1   Beat the eggs well with a good pinch of salt. Put the chocolate pieces into a blender or food processor and pulse briefly to break them up.

2   In a small pan, heat the cream to boiling point and pour it over the chocolate in the blender container. Pulse again to dissolve the chocolate, and then add the beaten eggs and the brandy. Pulse all the ingredients together briefly to combine.

3   Pour into individual ramekins, tapping them down gently on a hard surface a few times to dislodge any bubbles that remain.

4   Chill in a refrigerator until set.

Serve either with a float of brandy or cream, or decorate to taste: I use a dusting of icing sugar. Crisp *cigarette russe* biscuits go well with this. I use sugar-dusted physalis as a plate decoration.

Rich-tasting simplicity!

Tarte au citron

It is no surprise that many different recipes for this classic lemon tart exist, each of which claims complete authenticity. Some tart shells are filled with a heart-stopping mixture of eggs and butter, while others enclose virtually a lemon *crème brûlée*.

The recipe below hails from Provence and incorporates the local speciality crop, almonds, to the lemon filling.

Serves 6

for the sweet pastry:
225 g flour
125 g butter
4 egg yolks
100 g caster sugar
a few drops of vanilla
  essence
pinch of salt

for the filling:
3 eggs
150 g caster sugar
grated zest and juice of
  2 lemons
150 g butter, melted
75 g of ground blanched
  almonds

1   Make the pastry and chill it until firm. Set a moderate oven (gas 4/350 F/180 C).

2   Bake the pastry 'blind' for 12 to 15 minutes, i.e. until set but not brown.

3   Remove from the oven, remove the weights (beans or whatever) and cool a little. Put a baking sheet in the oven to heat up.

4   Meanwhile beat the eggs with the sugar to 'ribbon' stage. Stir in the lemon rind and juice followed by the melted butter and ground almonds.

5   Pour the mixture into the pastry shell and cook on the baking sheet for about 20–25 minutes until the top of the filling is golden brown and set. (*Beware!* Protect the top of the dish from burning. Sugar 'catches' easily.)

The tart is ideally served warm with a little chilled *crème fraîche* as an accompaniment.

Umm-Ali ('mother of all')

Although based on pastry, this is *almost* the Arabic answer to classic Western bread-and-butter pudding, and is extremely popular. When filming in Egypt the cast and crew of the BBC's *Fortunes of War* found it quite addictive!

Serves 6

350 g cooked puff pastry
50 g pistachio nuts,
  chopped
50 g toasted flaked
  almonds
1½ tbsp lemon juice

300 ml milk
150 g sugar
pinch of cinnamon
1 egg, beaten
2 tsp rose water
8 fl oz single cream

1   Preheat the oven to gas 5/375 F/190 C. Butter a large glass baking dish and crumble the cooked puff pastry into it. Mix in the nuts and the lemon juice.

2   Heat together the milk, the sugar and cinnamon to scalding, and then slowly add the beaten egg.

3   Pour this light custard over the mixture in the dish, and sprinkle with rose water. Top the dish with the cream and bake for about 30 minutes or until golden.

Serve warm, with a little fresh cream.

Duke of Cambridge tart

This recipe is from the Duke of York Inn, Iddesleigh, Devon, remembered from my time filming on *Tarka the Otter* along the River Torridge. Baked slowly in the local pub's AGA cooker, this is a blissful, gently toffee'd delight.

for the pastry:
225 g plain flour
100 g fine ground almonds
150 g butter
1 egg
100 g caster sugar
½ tsp vanilla essence

for the filling:
150 g butter
150 g caster sugar
6 egg yolks, beaten
2–3 oz candied peel
a few glacé cherries
a handful of muesli flakes (optional)

1   Prepare an 8–9 inch pastry tin and line it with the pastry, having chilled it for half an hour or so.
2   Bake blind for about 12 minutes, remove the weights and allow to cool. Sprinkle the peel, cherries and muesli (if using) over the pastry case and set aside.
3   Over a medium low heat gradually bring the butter, sugar and egg yolks to boiling point in a saucepan. Watch out

that the mixture doesn't burn, and beware spits from the pan.

4   Pour this mixture over the pastry case and its contents and cook in a slow oven (gas 2/300 F/150 C) for about an hour and a half. NB: Timing is approximate, but the tart should be caramelised gently, not browned to a frazzle.

Serve hot (or even better cold when there's a light toffee texture on the tongue!), with a dollop of chilled *crème fraîche* alongside.

Rosemary and saffron cheesecake

A deliciously fragrant dessert recipe from Marie-Pierre Moine's *Aromatic Kitchen.*

for the base:
about 15 digestive biscuits, crushed
4 oz melted butter plus a little more for the tin
1 tbsp dried rosemary
2 oz caster sugar

for the cheesecake:
1 lb curd cheese (or light Philadelphia cream cheese)

3½ oz caster sugar
2 sprigs fresh rosemary, snipped fine
2½ tsp genuine liquid vanilla extract
3 large eggs, separated
pinch of saffron strands
9 fl oz chilled *crème fraîche*
icing sugar, to taste

1   Butter an 8-inch loose-bottomed cake tin and line it with baking parchment.

2 Crush the biscuits until finely crumbed and add the dried rosemary, the sugar and the melted butter; spread the mixture into the prepared tin. Chill well.

3 Preheat an oven to gas 5/375 F/190 C – or adjust AGA shelves to allow only moderate heat.

4 Blend together two-thirds of the cheese with the caster sugar, fresh rosemary, half the vanilla extract, the saffron[*] and the egg yolks until blended.

5 Beat the egg whites to soft peaks and fold them thoroughly into the mixture.

6 Tip into the tin, and bake for 20 minutes.

7 Allow to cool completely and chill for 2 hours.

8 Preheat the oven to gas 8/450 F/230 C.

9 Whisk the *crème fraîche* with the icing sugar to taste, the remaining curd cheese and the rest of the vanilla extract. Spread this over the cake and bake for 10–12 minutes until slightly coloured. Cool completely, then chill for at least 4 hours before serving.

---

[*] The author suggests infusing the saffron in a tablespoon of very hot water, but I'd suggest simply grinding the strands to fine powder so as to avoid flecks of yellow in the cheese mixture.

Italian prune and chocolate cake with espresso coffee syrup

I am not a chocoholic myself, but this recipe from Ursula Ferrigno's *Italy Sea to Sky* sounded so very good I was tempted to make it – and it is quite exceptionally luxurious.

Serves 8

200 g ready-stoned prunes,
  halved
4 tbsp Armagnac or
  Cognac
200 g superfine dark
  chocolate, in pieces
25 g top quality cocoa
  powder
175 g dark muscovado
  sugar

4 large free-range egg
  whites
75 g plain flour (I used
  'Tipo 00')

for the espresso syrup:
1 tsp espresso coffee, very
  finely ground
25 g caster sugar
1 tbsp lemon juice

1   First soak the halved prunes in the brandy for about 2
    hours, or until the spirit has been absorbed.

2   Preheat oven to gas 5/375 F/190 C – or arrange 2 AGA shelves in baking oven to cover the cake while cooking. Line a 20 cm (8-inch) springform baking tin with parchment paper.

3   Put the chocolate pieces, the cocoa, 150 g of the dark sugar and 150 ml (5 fl oz) of boiling water into a large mixing bowl. Stir until melted and glossily smooth.

4   In a separate bowl, whisk the egg whites until stiff and gradually incorporate the remaining sugar, whisking it in. Sift the flour over the mixture, folding it in gently with a metal spoon until it is fully incorporated.

5   Gently incorporate about a quarter of this egg white mixture into the chocolate mixture and stir well, then pour the chocolate mixture into the remaining egg whites and carefully fold in until the texture becomes loose. Pour into the prepared tin.

6   Scatter the prunes over the top (they will sink into the cake mixture), then bake for around 30 minutes. The sponge will rise and firm up around the prunes. The cake will sink a little in the tin as it cools out of the oven.

7   For the syrup: Place the coffee and sugar in a small heavy-based saucepan with the lemon juice and 150 ml (5 fl oz) of cold water. I also add any soaking liquid left over from the prunes. Heat gently, making sure the sugar has dissolved. Bring back to the boil and cook for 3–5 minutes until the mixture thickens and becomes a bit syrupy. Strain it, and serve spooned over the cake.

Spiced apple tart with almonds and a Calvados sabayon sauce

I adapted this recipe from Adlard's in Norwich. It looks more complicated than it actually is, and is well worth the effort.

Serves 6

4 dessert apples (I use
  Cox's orange pippin)

for the pastry:
225 g plain flour
100 g fine ground almonds
150 g butter
1 egg
125 g fine sugar
  (caster sugar)
1 tsp vanilla essence

for the almond paste:
75 g unsalted butter
150 g granulated sugar
½ a vanilla pod
1 level tsp ground
  cinnamon
125 g blanched chopped
  almonds

for the sabayon sauce:
2 egg yolks
1 tbsp caster sugar
1 dessertsp Calvados
6 tbsp dry white wine

1   Peel, core and coarsely chop the apples. Reserve.

2   Put the flour, butter and ground almonds in a bowl and work them together as you would for a short or fingertip pastry. In another bowl beat together the egg, sugar and the vanilla essence until very pale and frothy. Add this to the flour, mixing together rapidly so as not to clog. It's a good idea to finish the pastry by kneading it gently on a floured board. Roll the pastry into a ball and wrap it up in clingfilm. Put it into a refrigerator to rest for about 2 hours.

3   When the pastry has rested sufficiently and is soft enough to roll out thinly, use it to line an 8-inch diameter flan ring or baking ring.

4   To make the vanilla/almond paste, first cream the butter and the sugar together evenly. Then, using a very sharp knife, cut a vanilla pod in half lengthwise and scrape out the fine black seeds inside. (An irresistible scent!) Add this black 'gunge' plus the powdered cinnamon to the butter and sugar mix, and then beat in the chopped almonds.

5   Fill the prepared pastry case with the diced apple and press out a circle of almond paste to cover the apple. My own sugar/almond mixture is usually pretty crumbly, so I just sprinkle it evenly over the top of the apples. Bake at an oven temperature of gas 6/400 F/200 C for about 40 minutes.

6   In a double saucepan (or, if you haven't got one, use a bowl which you can place over a pan of barely simmering water) whisk together all the sauce ingredients for a few minutes over the heat until the mixture forms a thick 'mousse'. Serve straight away poured over the warm (*not* hot) tart.

Tarte aux myrtilles Alsacienne

While blueberries or bilberries are now available all year round in UK supermarkets, air-freighted from their scattered places of origin, the harvesting season in the Vosges begins in mid August and continues until the end of September.

The following recipe adapts very well to blackberries, too.

Serves 6

200 g sweet shortcrust
  pastry
3 tbsp fresh white
  breadcrumbs
500 g bilberries
  (blueberries)

6 tbsp whipping cream
4–5 tbsp caster sugar
1 tbsp plain flour
2 eggs
½ tsp powdered cinnamon
  (see note on next page)

1   Roll out the pastry to fit a 10-inch quiche tin and bake blind.
2   Sprinkle the base with the fresh breadcrumbs and cover with the blueberries, then put in a gas 6/400 F/200 C oven for about 15 minutes.

3   Meanwhile, whisk together the cream, the eggs, the flour and cinnamon* in a bowl. Remove the tart from the oven and pour the custard mixture over the fruit.

4   Return the tart to the oven for a further 15 minutes or until the custard is set.

I reckon this tart is best served either tepid or cold, when a little icing sugar can be sprinkled over.

---

* My own addition of a discreet amount of cinnamon (a spice well used by Alsatian cooks) seems to 'lift' the tart into another dimension without encroaching on the fruit flavours.

Portuguese 'pudim' of almonds and port

Serves 4–6

225 g ground almonds
300 ml milk, boiling
1 cup sugar
150 ml ruby port

3 eggs
3 egg whites
3 tbsp sugar

1   Sprinkle the 3 tbsp of sugar evenly on the bottom of a flameproof mould and place it over heat until the sugar melts and caramelises. Be careful not to let it burn as this will result in a bitter flavour. Leave it to cool until set.

2   Combine the almonds, cup of sugar and port in a basin and add the boiling milk. Let the mixture stand for about ten minutes.

3   Whip the eggs and egg whites together, and add to the mixture, gently stirring them in.

4   Pour this mixture into the prepared mould, cover it, and place in a larger heatproof pan with water. Cover the larger pan and steam the mould until the mixture sets. I normally allow 45 minutes to 1 hour's steaming.

5   Leave to cool completely, unmould and serve.

Crema Catalana

This is from Simon Hopkinson's *Roast Chicken and Other Stories* – a 'must-have' cookbook – and is one of my occasional alternatives to a straight *crème brûlée*. *Crema Catalana* bears more similarity to the ubiquitous Spanish *flan* as, apart from the flavourings, there is no caramelised sugar-brittle topping. The taste is subtle but quite distinctive. Some may find the hint of fennel 'aniseed' a bit strange in a dessert, but I think it tastes authentically 'Spanish'.

500 ml double cream
150 ml whole milk
1 tbsp crushed fennel
  seeds
1 vanilla pod, split down
  its length

rind of a lemon, grated
rind of a small orange,
  grated
3 egg yolks
90 g sugar

1   Pre-heat oven to gas 1/275 F/140 C.
2   Gently heat together the cream, milk, fennel seeds, split vanilla pod, and the lemon and orange rinds. Once this comes up to the boil give it a whisk to disperse the vanilla seeds, then take off the heat and leave to infuse for about half an hour.

3   Whisk together the egg yolks and sugar until thick and then strain the cooled cream infusion and add to the beaten eggs and sugar. Whisk again to combine, then leave to stand for 10 minutes or so. By this time the froth will have stabilised on top which can then be skimmed off.

4   Pour into ramekins (or individual Spanish *flan* pottery dishes – should you happen to have any to hand), place in a bain-marie of cold water and cook in the oven for about an hour or until set.

5   Chill thoroughly – a few hours or even overnight.

Pasteis de Belém

These *wonderful* little custard tarts are well known throughout Portugal and have their origins in an ancient recipe created by monks at the Monastery of S. Geronimo in the Belém district of Lisbon. Home-made versions may not be quite as shapely as the ones served in a famous café across from the monastery, but oh! – the *taste*... All right, settle down everybody!

puff pastry dough
(I cheat and buy it ready
  made these days)

for the filling:
5 fl oz (140 g) single cream
4 egg yolks
2½ oz (75 g) caster sugar
icing sugar and powdered
  cinnamon, to dust over

1   Prepare the filling by beating the egg yolks and sugar together in a bowl until thick, adding the cream gradually. Make sure it is beaten in well and then transfer to a saucepan or double boiler and bring the mixture to a gentle simmering heat, stirring until a thick custard is obtained. Leave to cool down completely.

2   Roll out the pastry as thinly as practicable and cut out rounds big enough to line patty or bun tins.

3   Chill the pastry-lined tins in a refrigerator for half an hour, then fill each patty with a good tablespoonful of the custard and bake in a hot oven for 8–10 minutes, or until the custard is browned on top and the pastry is golden. Cool, and dust with icing sugar and cinnamon – the traditional finishing touch.

Olive oil and Vin Santo cake

5 egg yolks
7 egg whites
1 cup demerara sugar
1 tbsp grated orange zest

½ tsp salt
1 cup sifted cake flour
½ cup Vin Santo
½ cup olive oil

1   Whisk egg yolks with the sugar. Beat in Vin Santo, olive oil and zest of orange.

2   Sift the flour and salt together and fold in carefully. Whisk up the egg whites and fold them into the mixture.

3   Pour the batter into a springform cake tin that has been brushed with olive oil and lined with a disc of bakewell paper. Bake for 20 minutes.

4   Turn oven off and leave to cool down for 10 minutes. Turn out and dust with icing sugar.

Wine:
Vin Santo, Villa di Vetrice.

My basic ice cream mixture

Serves 4

4 egg yolks
100 g sugar
either 600 ml of half
   cream, or 300 ml each of

whipping cream and
full-cream milk
½ vanilla pod, cut down its
   length

1   Beat the egg yolks and sugar together in a bowl until the mixture is very pale and running in ribbons.

2   Heat the cream and split vanilla pod until just below boiling point.

3   Combine the hot cream with the egg/sugar mixture, stirring until well incorporated, and transfer to a clean saucepan.

4   Put the saucepan over gentle heat, stirring constantly until the mixture thickens.

5   Remove from heat and allow to cool completely, giving the mixture an occasional stir. Strain through a fine sieve, and freeze either using an ice-cream churn or in a container in the deep freeze itself. (If adopting the latter course, keep turning the sides of the mixture into the centre as it freezes to ensure an even consistency.)

Clove ice cream

Having tasted her own brilliant clove ice cream, I plucked up courage to ask top restaurateur Sally Clarke how she made it. She said simply: 'Make some ice cream and put some cloves in it.' A sound principle, though detail was lacking!

What follows is my own approach, and though I say it myself it produces remarkably similar results to her own.

1. Make up a little bag of fine muslin in which you have put ½ tsp of powdered cloves.
2. Follow the basic ice cream recipe on page 193 and, at the beginning of stage 4, steep the bag of powdered cloves in the custard mixture as it heats up to thicken, pressing it against the side of the saucepan occasionally with a small spoon to extract the flavours.
3. Remove the bag once the custard mixture is cold. The ice cream should be the palest *café au lait* colour.

Heavenly when served with fresh strawberries!

Pine-honey ice cream with fruits of the forest

This recipe comes from the Vosges region of France, and is one of the simplest ice-cream dishes possible, requiring neither cooking of custards nor any churning in a machine.

Serves 4–6

3 egg yolks, organic
1 whole egg
6 fl oz pine honey (I use
   dark Greek honey)
10 fl oz whipping cream

to serve:
a mix of raspberries,
   blackberries, bilberries
   and strawberries; I
   suspect little alpine
   strawberries alone might
   be wonderful alongside
   when in season
caster sugar

1   Beat the egg yolks, egg and honey together with an electric mixer until as light and fluffy as possible. The original recipe suggests 'until tripled in bulk' – but this may be a counsel of perfection!

2   In a separate bowl whip the cream until it stands in soft peaks, and gently fold it into the egg/honey mixture using a metal spoon.

3   Freeze in ramekins or other small containers, or even yogurt pots.

Serve with a mix of fruits of the forest alongside to which you have added *just* enough caster sugar to take off the acidic edge. Perfect!

Basil ice cream

The intriguingly sweet clove-like scent of fresh basil infuses this ice-cream. The use of vanilla in the basic custard mixture as given earlier is optional.

1   Follow the basic ice cream recipe given on page 193 but reducing the quantity of sugar to 75 g.
2   At the beginning of stage 4, add a good fistful of roughly chopped fresh basil to the cream, letting the leaves steep in the ice-cream custard right the way through until the mixture has cooled down. Basil leaves blacken as they meet heat, but don't worry – they won't colour the custard.
3   Once the thickened custard is cool enough, pour it through a sieve to filter out the leaves, and freeze in the usual way.

I remember once serving this intriguingly flavoured ice cream 'blind' to a magistrate who guessed – incorrectly – that it was cannabis!

Lavender & Greek honey ice cream

1   Follow the basic recipe on page 193 but, in stage 1, beat the egg yolks with 6 oz of clear honey instead of the sugar. (Greek honey is wonderfully full-flavoured.)

2   At stage 2 omit the vanilla and add 4 heads of lavender flowers... certainly no more, as the aromas are quite pungent. Sieve the heads out at stage 5, just before freezing the mixture.

Variations:

This method adapts to many other flavouring agents including scented geranium leaves (don't use more than 4... their flavour is also quite pungent); or Earl Grey Tea etc. The choice of flavourings is endless... and it is yours!

Note:

In general, ensure ice-cream flavourings are positive before you freeze the ice cream, as the freezing process can tend to mask them slightly.

Rosemary-infused chocolate ice cream

a finger-length sprig of
  fresh rosemary
⅓ cup cocoa powder (the
  unsweetened kind)
½ cup caster sugar

½ cup condensed milk
1½ cups full-cream milk
1 vanilla pod, split
  lengthways
1 cup heavy cream, chilled

1   Lightly bruise the fresh rosemary with a rolling pin, and
    put it in a measuring jug.

2   In a heavy-bottomed saucepan put together the cocoa
    powder, the sugar, the condensed and full-cream milk
    and the split vanilla pod. Bring them to the boil and then
    allow to simmer very gently for at least five minutes,
    stirring all the while.

3   Once the mixture has cooked through and cooled just a
    little, strain the liquid into the measuring jug with the
    rosemary. When completely cold stir in the chilled heavy
    (or whipping) cream and transfer the jug to a refrigerator
    to chill for a few hours, preferably overnight.

4   During this time the rosemary aromatics will infuse the
    chocolate mixture, but it's worth testing to see if the

flavour is strong enough – leave to infuse further if not to taste.

5   When ready, take out the rosemary sprig and, in order to remove any odd leaves, sieve the chocolate mixture into an ice-cream maker. Churn for about 20 minutes. Transfer this semi-frozen mixture into a polythene freezer box and freeze until required. (If you don't have an ice-cream churn, simply put the mixture in freezer trays and turn the sides into the middle occasionally while freezing.)

Note:
If you can use the highly aromatic Tuscan rosemary, so much the better. Its leaves are slightly broader than common rosemary, and there's an added flavour dimension akin to dark Greek honey!

Saffron ice cream

Serves 4–6

1 pint full-cream milk
good pinch of saffron
  threads

7 egg yolks (large eggs)
150 g caster sugar
250 ml whipping cream

1   Bring the milk to the boil in a saucepan. Meanwhile, pound the saffron threads in a pestle and mortar – or use a pinch of powdered saffron instead.

2   Add the saffron to the hot milk... you may have to put a tablespoonful or two of the milk into the mortar to extract residues of colour/flavour.

3   Beat the egg yolks together with the sugar. The mixture will eventually turn pale and form frothy 'ribbons'.

4   Gradually add the hot saffron-infused milk, stirring well.

5   Return this mixture to either a double-boiler, the bottom section filled with hot water, or to a separate pan over a low heat. Stir constantly until the mixture thickens.

6   Add the whipping cream, stirring it in well, and then allow the mixture to get completely cold.

7   Transfer to an ice-cream maker and churn until frozen. Alternatively, put it into a shallow tray and freeze for

about 40 minutes; remove and whisk the sides into the middle. Repeat the process a couple of times and then allow to freeze until firm.

Coffee and cardamom ice cream

First make the basic ice-cream custard mixture (see page 193), omitting the vanilla.

for the flavouring:
6 heaped tsp of dark 'continental roast' instant coffee granules

3 heaped tsp dessert chocolate powder (I use Charbonnel & Walker)
1 tsp of cardamom seeds, ground fine

1   Using a pestle and mortar, extract the seeds from about a tablespoonful of cardamom pods – this should render around a teaspoonful of seeds. Put these seeds in a grinder and whizz until they become a fine powder.

2   Add the ground cardamom seeds plus the coffee granules and the chocolate powder to the cream in the pan, mix well to dissolve and allow everything to come up to just below boiling point.

3   Pour the mixture onto the bowl of beaten egg yolk/sugar (basic recipe), and mix well.

4   Transfer to a clean pan over low heat, and stir until the mixture thickens. Remove from the heat; allow to cool down completely, and churn in an ice-cream maker.

Brown bread ice cream

Despite its somewhat pedestrian title, this is something special, and it doesn't rely on the usual ice-cream 'custard' but on whipped cream and brown breadcrumbs caramelised with an equal quantity of muscovado sugar.

300 ml of double cream
1 oz vanilla sugar
100 g stale brown
  breadcrumbs

100 g muscovado sugar

to serve:
brandy or rum

1   Lightly whip the cream together with the vanilla sugar, chill, and churn in an ice-cream machine until semi-hardened – or put into a tray in the freezer and turn the sides into the middle occasionally until you get the correct consistency.

2   Meanwhile, make day-old brown bread slices into crumbs and put into a lightly oiled baking tray together with the muscovado sugar. Mix well together, and either put under a grill or into a gas 6/400 F/200 C oven so that the sugar caramelises with the bread... You'll need to watch carefully, as you don't want the sugar to burn and become bitter.

3   Once the bread and the sugar have fused together, remove from the grill or oven and allow to cool completely. Break up the mixture into crumbs again. Introduce the caramelised crumbs to the semi-frozen whipped cream to combine evenly, and refreeze until required.

4   If required, pour a spoonful of brandy or rum over each serving portion. As a good match, hand brandysnaps alongside.

Elderflower ice cream

This can be made at any time of the year, as either a commercial or (in season) a home-made elderflower cordial is employed for flavouring.

Serves 6

300 ml full-cream milk
6 medium egg yolks
100 g caster sugar

300 ml Jersey or clotted
   cream, or a mixture of
   the two
200 ml elderflower cordial

1   Bring the milk to boiling point in a heavy saucepan, then remove from heat. Whisk the egg yolks and sugar together in a bowl, pour in the milk and whisk well.

2   Return the mixture to the pan and cook over a low heat for about 5 minutes, stirring constantly with a whisk. Make sure the mixture doesn't come to the boil. Remove from the heat and whisk in the cream and the elderflower cordial.

3   Leave to cool completely, then churn in an ice-cream machine until thickened. Decant into a clean container and place in the freezer.

Alphabetical list of recipes